HOW TO MAKE YOUR FIRST MILLION

Books by Lillian Too also available from Rider

Essential Feng Shui
Creating Abundance with Feng Shui

HOW TO MAKE
YOUR FIRST
MILLION

Lillian Too

RIDER

LONDON · SYDNEY · AUCKLAND · JOHANNESBURG

1 3 5 7 9 10 8 6 4 2

Copyright © Lillian Too 2000
Lillian Too has asserted her right to be identified as Author of this work.

Published in 2000 by Rider,
an imprint of Ebury Press, Random House,
20 Vauxhall Bridge Road, London SW1V 2SA
www.randomhouse.co.uk

Random House Australia (Pty) Limited
20 Alfred Street, Milsons Point, Sydney,
New South Wales 2061, Australia

Random House New Zealand Limited
18 Poland Road, Glenfield,
Auckland 10, New Zealand

Random House South Africa (Pty) Limited
Endulini, 5A Jubilee Road,
Parktown 2193, South Africa

The Random House Group Limited Reg. No. 954009

Papers used by Rider Books are natural, recyclable products made from
wood grown from sustainable forests.

Typeset by SX Composing DTP, Rayleigh, Essex
Printed and bound by Mackays of Chatham

A CIP catalogue record for this book is available from the British Library

ISBN 0-7126-0734-X

CONTENTS

INTRODUCTION

I did not begin my career with the aim of becoming a million dollar woman. Far from it. I began working life in the same way many of my contemporaries did, as a humble executive officer, fresh out of university and eager to make my own living. I did not even begin work in the private sector. Indeed, my first real job was with a government agency – MIDA (the Malaysian Industrial Development Authority, then known as FIDA- the Federal Industrial Development Authority). But unlike most other government agencies, FIDA was both dynamic and fast moving. During my five years there, I met hundreds of local and foreign business people, all keen to set up manufacturing operations in Malaysia. Those were wonderful learning years and the first glimmerings of interest in commerce and business management took root in my mind.

Many of Malaysia's successful entrepreneurs, business tycoons and corporate bigwigs earned their spurs at FIDA. I suppose like me, they too were inspired by the business people who walked through the corridors of the agency, discussing ideas for business, getting licenses for new factories, looking for suitable locations, setting up plants, applying for tax incentives and tariff protection and just generally taking advantage of the country's huge potential for growth.

It was to take me about ten years to achieve career success as a corporate woman, and then another five to become a six-figure business woman. I took time off to gain an MRA at the Harvard Business School, followed by a spell as a financial analyst in a merchant bank, before landing a job with the Hong Leong Group. While with them, I accepted a variety of professional assignments including a transfer to Hong Kong to run a recently acquired bank there – the Grindlays Dao Heng Bank – and landed smack in the middle of Hong Kong's worst banking crisis!

Hong Kong became the catalyst for me. It was there that I made the leap from corporate woman to businesswoman. It was there that I directed all my energies, all my creativity to packaging the deal that eventually gave me the freedom to pursue my own dreams.

I left my safe and secure job and plunged into the world of business. When I did it, I was optimistic and very determined, but also very very scared. I knew that if I failed, not only would I lose my hard earned capital – which I had spent years saving – but worse, I knew it would quite shatter my confidence. However, I was also confident that if I worked at it, if I did not allow my determination to falter, I would succeed. I started, therefore, with a tremendous and uncompromising belief in myself. In short, I was hungry for success.

So, you see, I did not become a millionaire overnight. Nor did most other financially successful people. Many of today's flourishing entrepreneurs have, like me, spent at least a part of their working life as corporate executives. Frequently they gave up safe and potentially lucrative corporate careers to pursue a different kind of success in the business world. And in the process ended up making more money than they ever dreamed possible.

Not many of them, especially the senior women executives and managers, have found it easy to juggle the demands on their time or attention. Women are usually denied the luxury of focusing single-mindedly on success at work. They tend to take on more domestic responsibilities and do not have the same priorities as men. Yet they have the same work ethic, often possess the same drive and manifest the same abilities and derive as much satisfaction from achieving success as men do.

The solution for many women is to parlay whatever skills, ideas and abilities they have into building their own business and becoming their own boss. The promise of greater financial rewards is only part of the story. What is even more enticing about making the decision to build your own business is the wonderful feeling which comes from setting your own pace, designing your business around your lifestyle, arranging flexibility of working hours and, most attractive of all, becoming truly financially independent.

But whatever your sex, you must really want to succeed. Determination generates the energies and strengths you will need to get started and to stay resilient. Confidence and positive self-expectancy will see you through many early difficulties. In essence, becoming a million-dollar person starts in the mind.

I am persuaded that everyone has the potential to succeed at whatever they set their mind to. The twelve chapters in this book will take you step-by-step through the basics of getting started in business, beginning with the hows of sourcing ideas and options and then evaluating their commercial viability.

Once an idea has been chosen, the next step is the formulation of a business plan, which gives form and substance to a money-making scheme. Getting started requires courage and conviction – crucial components in the money making process. If you want to become rich, you must be action-oriented; you must take the initiative and seize the opportunity. You must not prevaricate and make excuses; nor allow self-doubts and fear of failure to seriously immobilise you.

The early years of building a business are fraught with problems. Things generally will, and do, go wrong. So you need to develop a success attitude and a success ethic from the start. Managing the initial stages however can be made easier when you know what to do and how to anticipate problems.

Watching your expenses, keeping simple accounts, managing the margins and keeping track of the bottom line – all of these skills can be learnt quite easily. More difficult is learning to make judgements, to make good decisions. This is especially true when things go wrong, when one is confronted with the unpleasant realities of the business world – dishonesty, unsupportive staff, unsympathetic bankers, difficult bureaucratic regulatory agencies, unreliable suppliers, and so forth.

Successful businesspeople learn very quickly to sift through the trivialities. They seldom have the time to either get petty or get their priorities confused. With persistence and a clear vision, eventually things will go right. Sales will take off. Routines will get established and over time a rhythm of success will be created. That is when thoughts of expansion, of new directions, of growth begin to look enticing.

Now the need to think strategically becomes crucial. Trade-offs need to be analysed and examined. Dilemmas caused by the clashing of priorities will have to be resolved. The moderately successful entrepreneur will always reach a stage when he or she is forced to take stock of various options and the sacrifices that need to be made. Thinking things through will make the options clearer and the decisions easier to make.

Thus Chapters 8 and 9 focus on two opposing options – buying a business and selling a business. These are followed by a whole chapter which deals with the creating of value. This is a key chapter, because when you reach a certain level of success, profits can be cashed in, in several ways, and the creation of value is how one makes the leap towards becoming a millionaire. There is thus more to business than merely making and selling products. In today's business environment, value-creation is the name of the game. Understand this, and you will be able to transform your business into a million dollar asset.

Chapter 11 focuses on the management of change – the need for and the processes and impact of change – while the final chapter highlights the difference between preserving the millions you make versus the risks you took at the start of it all. Preservation of capital and maximising gains represent two different strategic directions, and once you have made it, once you have something to lose, your idea and attitude towards risk-taking will change.

But by then it doesn't really matter, because you will have made your million dollars . . . many times over!

Finally, for those of you interestested in oriental philosophy, the appendices contain some foolproof feng shui tips which will undoubtedly increase your own success, and that of your business.

Chapter One

IDEAS AND OPTIONS

Mark McCormack is probably not a name many of you are familiar with. He is the founder of the sports management industry. He is the man behind the millions made by golfers Arnold Palmer and Jack Nicklaus and tennis players Chris Evert and Martina Navratilova. Here's how he described his beginning:

> In the early 1960s I founded a company with less than $500 in capital and gave birth to an industry – the sports management and sports marketing industry. Today that company has grown into the International Management Group (IMG), with offices around the world and several hundred million dollars in annual revenues.

A more recent success story is that of Bill Gates, founder of the hugely successful computer software company, Microsoft, and probably the world's youngest and most successful self-made billionaire. McCormack parlayed an idea into a phenomenal new industry, while Gates commercialised a fantastic talent. McCormack sold a service, Gates sold a product. Both are business stories that can really inspire.

Successful businesses germinate in the minds of people with creative ideas: a new way of making something, a new way of packaging something, a new way of selling something, a new way of organising something . . . even, a new way of communicating something. Ideas spring from an infinite variety of sources. You can build a successful business around a product, around a new technology or around a service.

Evaluate skills or knowledge which you possess. An ability to cook delicious curries can give birth to a great curry powder business. A skill with a musical instrument can lead to the setting up of a specialised retail outlet. A new invention can be the nucleus of a commercial enterprise. Having excellent dress sense can be the inspiration for a chain of boutiques. A good organiser can package a whole variety of businesses, such as organising and providing security services or temporary office staff or an inner-city courier and delivery service. A love of flowers or a skill at flower arrangement can lead to a florist shop or supplying floral arrangements and plants to corporate offices and hotels, or even the manufacture of artificial silk flowers. Hong Kong's richest man, Li Ka Shing, started his business empire selling plastic flowers! Almost anything can be the seed of a good idea.

GETTING FOCUSED

One good way of generating business ideas is to talk about them with likeminded friends or relatives. But discussions of this kind must be *focused*. This is the key to moving your ideas on beyond the talking stage. You must organise your thoughts. First, think through the type of business you might be good at running. What special talents, skills or contacts do you have which will give you a competitive edge?

Consider this simple categorisation of businesses:

- production – making your own product to sell
- retailing – setting up a retail shop to sell products
- trading or wholesaling – buying from one and selling to another
- distribution – selling and delivering products to retail outlets
- services – providing a specialised service to other companies

Each of these types of business offers a broad variety of permutations in terms of organisation and structure. Focused thinking allows you to zero in on each of them, so that you can discard the options that do not appeal to you, or feel are beyond your abilities/ resources.

Next, having identified the type of business you want to start, ask yourself some very basic questions:

- Do you have the skill/knowledge/expertise to

manage the business?

- What special ability/contacts/ competitive advantage will you have?
- How much concentrated time can you devote to the business?
- Will you do everything yourself or will you have partners?
- Will you do everything in-house or will you use subcontractors?
- Are you starting from scratch or taking over an existing business?
- Do you feel confident about the idea so far?
- Is it a very competitive business?

Thinking through ideas along these lines will further reduce your options. It will also help refine the idea(s). If in doubt, seek advice from friends. If you require more information, take the trouble to seek out and talk to people already in the trade or industry you are thinking of entering. Do a lot of reading.

Keep abreast of new start-up situations. Your idea may be based on a franchise which has been offered to you or on a special advantage you have because of a special contact. It may come from a large order received from a company, local or overseas, or from a unique opportunity that just fell into your lap. Whatever the source, the next stage is to assess the commercial viability of the business idea. Is it practical? Will there be a demand for your product/service? And if not, can you create a demand?

MONEY, MONEY, MONEY . . .

Before plunging into any business venture, look very seriously at the basic financial aspects. You don't need to be an accountant or a graduate or an executive to cut through an idea and reduce it to numbers. But you do need commonsense, an honest approach and a certain determination and resilience. A checklist of the items to calculate does help.

Remember that when you start a business, every cent that goes out comes from your own pocket. Expenses have a nasty way of piling up and eating into your capital. To determine the risk of this happening, here's what you must calculate from the very beginning:

INCOME

Where is the income coming from?

List *all* the sources of income. How reliable is this income? Remember, income is not just sales. It is cash sales or if credit is given, it is collected sales revenue. Many trading businesses are notorious for the difficulties encountered in collecting. Unreliable income revenues can kill a business, so beware of this particular risk. The best business ideas are those where you really can identify a good market, where you can be reasonably sure of the income. Bear this in mind when evaluating ideas.

START-UP COSTS

Itemise all the expenditure required just to get started; then see if you can afford it. Include rental of office or premises, deposits on utilities, renovations, carrying of initial inventory (if any), and any other costs that are unique to your business. Remember that start-up costs are known as 'sunk' costs. If your business flourishes, you can depreciate start-up costs against income revenues. If your business fails, most of this money is lost unless you can sell the business to someone else.

OPERATING EXPENSES

Once the business gets going, what are the major and minor expenses, the fixed and the variable costs? Do not worry about the accounting terms. Just list all the expenses you can identify. You can easily subcontract the keeping of accounts, all company secretarial work and other logistics to a firm of accountants. For the moment, just focus on the viability of the business by knowing well before you start how much money you require to cover all your expenses for the first six months. Yes, it often can take this long before you start to see money flowing in (unless you are engaged in what is known as a 'cash business', such as a shop or other retail operation). A business takes time to build up, so do make sure that you are prepared for at least six months of calculated expenses. Otherwise you could have 'cash flow problems'. Operating expenses can be classified as fixed or variable. Fixed expenses are those which you have to pay for whether or not you make any sales. Variable expenses are things you pay for depending on how much you sell.

When you have more than one good idea, go for the one with which you are most sure of the income revenues. In the ultimate analysis, irrespective of size, reliability of the sources of income revenue is the single most important factor to consider. Remember you can only have a business if it can generate income. When you can be reasonably sure of money coming in, then you can go on to the next stage and start to look at managing profit margins. Which is where the business plan comes in. But while you are still deciding on what business to be in, make sure you think through carefully how successfully you can sell your product or service.

Chapter Two

YOUR-MONEY MAKING STRATEGY

We live in prosperous, exciting and fast-changing times. New technologies are unlocking new horizons for aspiring millionaires. At no time since the Second World War have the opportunities been broader, or so exciting and enticing. In the first chapter, we focused on ideas. Next, I suggest you pause and look around you, at the new products that have come on the market, at the amazing explosion of Internet technology and usage, at the rise of electronic gimmickry and electronic commerce, at the burgeoning commercial activity that is sweeping across the world. Most of all, look at the sudden appearance and dominance of virtual companies – companies that exist literally in thin air – somewhere in the electronically transmitted world of virtual commerce. This is but one of the many changing dimensions of today's world.

If you want to become a millionaire and enjoy financial success you must take note of this new world and carve out a place for yourself within it. In business jargon, this means creating a niche for yourself, your company, your skills or your professional expertise. Your special niche can serve your local area, region or country. It can even be global. You decide the magnitude of your ambitions. In this allow your right brain freeflow. I always say, how can your great dreams come true if you don't dare to dream them in the first place.

Remember that to become a success, there is nothing stopping you except your own mind and your own desires. This tenet has become ever more true as we approach the new millennium. Global communication and international market penetration is now available at the push of a computer button. There is a stunning expansion of spending power. Observe it, and let your observations inspire you to carve out a share of this new abundance for yourself. Despite downturns and pauses to the economic pulse, the world is transforming in thousands of new directions. Let these new developments arouse tantalising possibilities in your mind. Do not put it off until tomorrow. Start investigating what I am saying now. Let the millionaire instinct inside you start to blossom.

POSITIVE THINKING

The next step in your exciting quest to make yourself rich is to take all the ideas spawned by your thinking mind a little further. Thus, first you dream, allowing your mind to flow, jotting down all your ideas and allowing your creativity free rein. Then, you put your ideas to the commercial test. This examines whether you really can transform just one of them into a profitable money-making venture.

The stakes should be high because it will be your decision whether or not to invest your time and money. When you start to craft your own business and career strategy, it will be *your* time and capital at risk.

The personal risks are what will make your adrenaline flow. Allow your thoughts to excite you. Feel the fear of taking the risks. Acknowledge that it is all a little scary. Then overcome your fears by thinking about the rewards, which can be limitless. Go with the flow!

Start by stacking as many of the cards in your favour as possible. Do this by mapping out exactly how you intend to commence, by identifying the things that need to be attended to and the arrangements that must be sorted out. You must assess how much capital you need (and have), how much risk you're prepared to take and how much time you're prepared to put into the new strategy you are formulating for your future. Some people also find it useful to give themselves a timeframe for success. I do. I usually expect to see some kind of real and positive result within eighteen months. But you should set your own pace.

Making money should be an enjoyable process. Never allow yourself to forget this. If you do, the obstacles and problems that crop up along the way will depress you to an extent that you will simply give up. And success is not for those who throw in the towel and get discouraged easily. Success is for those who learn from every bad experience and every problem encountered. And you can only maintain this positive attitude if you are genuinely enjoying what you do. It is your belief in your objective and in yourself that will sustain you through the hard times.

MAKING A BUSINESS PLAN

Planning is simply a matter of thinking systematically and using your commonsense. Even the most sophisticated business plans ultimately boil down to commonsense, except that in the corporate world they are couched in the language of business and expressed in terms of numbers and standardised financial formats. Those with a training in finance or management or with work experience in the business world will find it easier to speak this language. But the lack of such a background should not stop you. Business terms quickly become second nature once you start to think in a businesslike way.

Your business plan should be a statement of the major activities you must undertake.

- Make forecasts of the start-up money required, the income to be expected and the expenses to be incurred; then quantify these forecasts. This is the hard part, but it forces you to discipline yourself and to think through your plan in a logical way, thereby engaging your left brain.
- Set out your program of action – the sequence and timing of work to be done.
- Determine how much and what type of manpower you need.
- Define targets for outputs, sales levels, quality, standards, costs and all other related aspects where performance needs to be monitored and measured.
- Plan workflows and specify the systems and procedures to be put in place.
- Estimate what stocks to buy, what materials to purchase and what subcontractors to use, and determine the sources of supply for these.
- Determine the physical facilities required, such as manufacturing, selling and office space (plus related machinery and equipment) and list possible locations/make of equipment.

- Finally reduce all of the above to numbers, to come up with some sort of financial budget that will form the essence of your business plan.

Planning is not something that can be completed in one day. It requires concentration and focused thinking. It combines all your ideas, and forces you to connect each of them together so that a cohesive blueprint becomes the eventual result of your efforts. Just the act of putting thoughts down on paper will make you see things you may have missed in the initial enthusiasm of the ideas stage. It is wonderful to be action-oriented, but the impulse to plunge in must always be tempered with a rational calculation of the financial aspect.

When you have thought through the above, sit back and consider whether anything has been left out. There is no foolproof recipe-type approach to business planning. Or, for that matter, to getting rich.

Every commercial enterprise is different and every entrepreneur is unique. So do personalise and customise your planning to suit your work style, your eccentricities and your belief systems. Let your plan work around you and for you. Allow for a certain amount of flexibility; recognise the possibility that implementation problems may force you to make changes and alterations to initial plans.

Planning must always allow for contingencies and unforeseen difficulties, which almost always cost money. Since it is impossible to anticipate everything, be prepared for unpleasant surprises and set aside what is generally referred to as a contingency sum which, as a rule of thumb, is calculated as 10–15 per cent of total initial capital required. You just might need this extra cushion.

When you are ready to finalise your business plan, let it comprise:

- a timeframe and a set of quantified financial targets, i.e. sales income and profits
- an action program expressed as quantified expenses and capital investments
- an analysis of the risks

Your business plan should tell you over a period of one year:

- how much sales revenue you can generate and collect
- what sort of average gross profit margin (GPM) you can hope to get
- what your total monthly and annual expenses will be
- what kind of initial capital outlay (or investment) you need to come up with
- what your monthly operating expenses and cost of goods (working capital) will be

ANALYSING RISK

Your business plan will zero in on the fundamental aspects of setting up a business. But to highlight the risk areas – what can go wrong and how this can translate into hard cash – requires further analysis.

SALES REVENUE

You will need to think through how you intend to market and sell your products or services. What and where is your market; who are your customers? Do you need to give credit? Will you have to take on the risk of bad debts? If the answer is yes, can you reduce the risk and how? If you decide not to give credit, by how much will your sales be affected? And if you can't sell your stock, how perishable is it? Jewellery can go up in value, but food items are perishable and have a short shelf-life, and clothing goes out of fashion.

GROSS PROFIT MARGIN (GPM)

Analyse this item carefully. We call it *gross* because this figure does not yet take into account your expenses. It refers merely to the difference between the selling price less the cost of the product. For example, if a dress is sold for $350 and it cost you $150, your gross profit margin per dress is $200 or 57 per cent of the selling price. Some businesses have higher GPMs than others.

Always remember that GPM is different from the mark-up. To get a GPM of 57 per cent the mark-up is times 2.3, meaning that you have priced your product at 2.3 times what it cost you, either to make or to buy from someone else. From this you can see that by analysing your GPM, you are in effect working out a pricing strategy – and your sales success depends on this strategy. In formulating strategy, you need to consider the competition, as well as your own operating expenses and overheads. Obviously the GPM must cover these – so the selling price must be high enough. Otherwise your business will not make a profit. On the other hand, don't price yourself out of the market.

In most franchises and the wholesaling of branded products, the retail selling price is usually fixed, and there is little room to manoeuvre. Many boutique businesses selling luxury branded items have to mark-up really high because of the low level of sales, so that even when high discounts are given, there is still a high GPM to cover high operating expenses. Do think through profit margins carefully. They go to the heart of a business and are what differentiate one business enterprise from another. Low GPM items/businesses must be compensated with high sales volume, so that the total sales revenue is enough to cover operating expenses and still show a profit. This is the rationale for most mass-market businesses, like supermarkets and consumer products.

OPERATING EXPENSES

These are *all* the expenses incurred by a business – rent, salaries, office expenses, utilities, advertising, printed matter, transport, travel, first-aid equipment, interest on loans, and so forth. The list is actually much longer than this, and how much you want to break it down further and categorise it is up to you but the thing to remember about operating expenses is that your GPM must more than cover these expenses, otherwise you will be making a loss. Do remember, however, that most actual costs are usually higher than forecast costs, so allow for a 10 per cent margin. Also, remember that each year costs will go up by at least the percentage of inflation, even if you don't expand.

CAPITAL INVESTMENT

This refers to the amount of capital you need to put into the business. It is calculated by estimating all your non-operating expenses, such as deposits on rentals and utilities, the cost of stock/inventory, and all other costs involved in setting up the business – the purchase of office equipment, transport facilities and so forth.

WORKING CAPITAL

You would be advised to set aside at least six months worth of your estimated operating expenses as working capital. Only when you start collecting revenues regularly each month can the business be considered self-financing.

If you go through the above conscientiously, it becomes easy to come to certain conclusions about how practical and sound your original business idea was. If the numbers don't look right, examine again the basis of your various assumptions in putting these numbers together. It is easy to get carried away and forecast a huge sales revenue. Remember that the amount of sales revenue you can get does depend a great deal on how big you want your business to be. This has to do with the capacity of your business. In the beginning, start small and limit your financial risk, because when you start, you do not yet know enough about the business and therefore will be unable to manage the risks involved.

Learn about the business first, so that you will then know how to reduce the risks, before taking on greater ones. Almost all self-made millionaires manage their initial financial risk with extreme care. Only when they understand the business they are in and know at least 60 per cent of the tricks of the trade, so to speak, do they allow themselves to grow and expand.

What all this means in business language is they watch their cash-flow very carefully. In simple language, this translates to being tight with money and making certain they do not allow themselves to become vulnerable to a shortage of cash.

Chapter Three

GETTING STARTED

Let's borrow some Tao wisdom from Lao-Tse, China's ancient sage:

> Begin difficult things when they are easy. Do great things when they are small. The difficult things of the world must once have been small. A thousand mile journey begins with the first step.

Getting rich starts with getting started. Getting started requires courage and confidence. By now, having worked out your numbers and your strategic gameplan, there is every reason to be confident, because you have already thought through all the things that you need to do. Getting started also means having to close the door to some things. You may have to quit a job, disentangle yourself from an existing circumstance and, most difficult, change some old habits and rearrange your lifestyle.

Confronting change like this can be traumatic, but how difficult coping with change is, depends entirely on you. There will definitely be well-meaning people around you who could cause you to have doubts and make you lose courage. Dump those people, at least until you are well on your way. Stick with those who will support you, that will bring out the best in you. If it is any consolation, think to yourself 'There is nothing bad in failing; there is everything good in trying and there is a more than fifty-fifty chance of succeeding, so I'm going to go for it.'

Sometimes events can suddenly crystallise a situation for you, making it easier for you to take the plunge. For instance, you may get fired from your job or bypassed for a promotion or lose out in some ridiculous office warfare. Adversity and a negative situation often bring out a passionate anger, which can be profitably channelled into a new direction.

If you're ready to begin making your first million dollars, now is the time to focus on practicalities and get started.

ARRANGING FUNDS

This is one of the first things to do. You can finance your business in one of several ways:

- entirely out of your own savings
- getting a loan from your husband/father/brother/cousin/friend/aunt
- inviting in a well-heeled partner, who may be a friend/classmate/soulmate
- applying for 'venture capital financing'
- applying for a bank loan, or
- through a mix of the all of the above, in various combinations

Getting the start-up finance together will be the first deal you make, and business is very much about making deals. It can be easy or difficult depending on many factors. Obviously if you have previously worked and built up credibility, or are able to demonstrate past successes in managing related businesses as a professional employee, you will have an easier time convincing banks and other financial institutions to make you a loan. Be prepared to discuss/explain your projections and business plan, and do have them nicely typed up and looking professional and impressive.

Most banks, however, are fairly conservative and you may be required to offer some kind of tangible asset or property to support your request for a loan. This could be a second mortgage on your house, or a personal guarantee from someone with good credit rating who believes in you, or a piece of land you might have inherited or purchased some years ago.

If, in the course of talking to banks and finance companies (and investigating alternatives), you meet up with pompous or haughty executives, do not be disheartened. Instead listen carefully to their observations and reactions, and also to the reasons given for any refusal. Learn from these reactions. Speak to several banks. When you first start out, you must have a thick skin and not let disappointments or refusals make you feel inadequate or rejected. In business, nothing is personal. So do not be too sensitive. In fact you should consider meeting difficult people during the early part of your pursuit of business success as valuable lessons in learning to cope. You should think of them as gems, since this gives you so much opportunity to practice patience (probably the most valuable asset to have in business and in life itself). Just make sure you do not get discouraged by silly bureaucracy or lose your temper with officialdom.

Usually, unless you are able to tap into some of the special funds that have been set up specifically to finance new ventures, your chance of success is at best only 50/50. But there is no harm trying, because you will learn a great deal from the exercise. It could give you a good idea of exactly how bankable you and your business ideas are, and make you rethink certain aspects of your plan.

Banks have a notorious reputation for being unhelp-ful towards new ventures. When I was in banking, we often joked that we would only lend to those who didn't really need to borrow, that we were fairweather friends, good to you only when you were already successful. This is not entirely untrue.

On no account try to 'bribe' a banker into lending you money. Whatever the outcome, keep lines of communication open with new banker friends. You may need to see the same people again when you have some sales figures to show. They could be more helpful then.

Meanwhile, go back to your figures. Calculate how much you are short, and see if you can realistically scale down your estimates. Be prepared to use your own funds/savings to start. If you are really short, seriously consider inviting a partner or an investor into the venture.

If you are able to arrange a loan, make sure it is sufficient (together with your own funds) to cover your estimated expenditure for a period of one year. Do note there are different types of loans – hire purchase to finance cars/trucks, leasing facilities to buy office, factory or other equipment, and so on. You can also sell your receivables (money owed to your business) to finance a company. This is called factoring. And you can arrange trade financing (known as trust receipts) to finance stock inventories.

Don't forget, suppliers usually offer between sixty to ninety days credit on inventory. This is known as trade credit, and although difficult to get during the early months, once you are seen as 'okay', you can negotiate for it. On the other hand, rentals and utilities require deposits and advance payments, which can often cover from one to three months.

CASH-FLOW

From the very start, watch your cash-flow closely. Make it a habit. Remember that cash-flow is *not* profit. Cash-flow is managing the cash coming in and going out.

Cash coming in is initially made up of equity capital and bank financing. As the business gets going you will have an additional source of cash and that is your 'cash from sales'. Later still, as your business begins to develop, you can also get cash from interest earned. Meanwhile, cash outflows are capital expenditures (buying equipment), operating expenses (rentals, salaries and so forth) and purchase of stocks and materials.

This is obviously a very simple treatment of cash-flow, but for the moment it should suffice. Making a habit of watching cash-flow right from the start is one of the best habits for an entrepreneur to develop, because it makes for conscious monitoring of a very crucial aspect of running a business.

SOME ADMINISTRATIVE DETAILS

I always advise my entrepreneur friends to set up or buy a ready-made limited company. This protects you by limiting any liabilities incurred by your business to the amount of paid-up capital (except for bank and other personal guarantees). Taking this strategy is being prudent.

Also, do keep your paid-up capital reasonably small. Most public companies only have $2 paid-up capital when they set up their subsidiaries, and only increase it when necessary. You can do the same. Besides, you can always 'advance' money to the company and treat it as a loan from a director (a loan from you to the company). Train yourself to think of the company as an entity in its own right, separate and distinct from you.

Keeping your paid-up capital low can give you some tax benefits too, which we need not go into yet. Speak to an accounting firm about setting up your company. Choose a medium-size reputable outfit. Let them take care of the accounting, the structuring of the company, all the board resolutions necessary for the opening of bank accounts and other legalities. Their charges are usually reasonable and most of them give excellent service. Build up a relationship with the executive handling your account. Remember that your accountants can also be your auditors and are an excellent source of sound advice later on, when your business gets bigger.

GETTING DOWN TO BUSINESS

Get down to the real business as soon as possible.

If you need to employ people, do so only when you really need them, and hire the best you can find and afford. Efficient employees are worth their weight in gold. Pay them a little above market rates or offer some kind of incentive related to performance, such as commissions and bonuses.

From the start, look for people who do not mind working for entrepreneurs. It is usually a good idea to employ someone you already know, someone who already has some kind of previous work experience with you. This makes life a lot easier. When I 'bought' my department store in Hong Kong, I took in many of my previous employees, including both my secretaries from my banking days. One became my group personnel manager and one became my fashion co-ordinator. I even brought my previous boutique manager from Kuala Lumpur to be my merchandiser. I never regretted those moves. They all proved to be loyal and dependable key people within my management team. I cannot overstress the great advantage of having people you can trust and depend on working for you.

Get your business premises set up as soon as possible. Speed is always vital, because time really is money. Rentals start the minute you sign on the dotted line. So do get going as soon as you can, focusing on the key tasks that need to be taken care of. Different businesses have different key tasks. You should know your key tasks by now. Most important, try to start generating income (making sales) as soon as possible.

Yes, there is a certain amount of urgency involved. A million things will go wrong. This is normal. The electricity supply could break down. The phones might not get installed on time. Your supplier could fail to deliver. The wonderful assistant you hired could change her mind and not show up. Meanwhile, your husband/wife might be acting up, your son start wetting his bed and your cleaner walk out! Take all these things in your stride. Believe me, in the end it will all come out right, if you just tackle problems systematically and keep your head. Deal with your business start-up problems as well as your domestic difficulties, but remember not to be so overwhelmed by all the nagging irritants as to forget the main business, or worse still succumb to the initial pressures of having to juggle your time and attention.

Back at the business, undertake all the marketing and selling preliminaries. Get the ball rolling. As you dispense with all the annoying trivialities of setting up business, you will soon get the knack of it. Before you know it, you will have established a daily rhythm, one that incorporates your new responsibilities with your domestic demands. Just make sure your routine includes a large chunk of time allocated to getting customers and clients. Because in the end, if you have the sales, if you can generate the income and get that humming nicely, your business will have got off to a great start.

Chapter Four

MANAGING THE START-UP

There are many clever definitions of what makes an entrepreneur. They have been described as people who turn business visions into business realities, as innovators who evoke demand, as makers of markets, as creators of capital, as developers of opportunity and as producers of new technology.

Successful entrepreneurs are spurred on by the strength of their vision and determination. They prevail not merely by understanding an existing situation in all its complexity, but by creating order out of disorder. They do it by tackling an infinite variety of difficult situations – almost always to an extent where their belief in themselves and their vision is greater than their knowledge at any given moment in time. In other words, if you have started your business and are presently engaged in getting your act together, do not be surprised or even discouraged when confronted with having to make decisions on matters you are as yet unfamiliar with.

Do believe me that the complexities of running a business, any business, require a composite of skills, expertise and knowledge not immediately available at the start of the venture. This is a universal experience of all entrepreneurs, managers and business people. You will absorb and assimilate many inter-related business skills as you move along. In management jargon, this is called moving up the learning curve. So never allow lack of knowledge to hold you back. When you need information, just go out and get it.

ATTITUDES FOR SUCCESS

Before addressing the critical areas that require attention in the building of a business, it helps to first cultivate and acquire certain specific attitudes which will speed up your progress along the learning curve, thereby vastly expanding your certainty of success. Just remember, even as you read this, that business success, as in all other fields of human endeavour, requires a determined pursuit of excellence. High achievers know that excellence is not an act but an attitude.

I believe this too, very strongly. I have devoted a great deal of time and effort over the years working at developing what I call winning attitudes. These are attitudes which affect the way I learn, the way I work, the way I approach a problem, the way my thought processes analyse a situation, the way I respond to people, the way I make judgements and the way I make decisions. I have identified eight success attitudes, which I believe to be invaluable for anyone who wants to be a high achiever. Let me share them with you:

- Being action-oriented rather than reaction-oriented, which means taking the initiative instead of always responding and reacting to situations.

- Taking control of circumstances to make things happen, never waiting for them to happen. Never wait to be pushed, always do the pushing.

- Always starting with your goal in mind in everything you do and never ever losing sight of it. Often, it is easy to lose sight of the wood for the trees and to allow one's daily work routines to cloud the ultimate objectives.

- Taking a solutions-oriented attitude rather than a blame seeker attitude. This means that when things go wrong, rather than wasting effort on seeing who is to blame and seeking excuses, you focus on what needs to be done to remedy the situation.

- Always thinking in terms of a win/win situation in your dealings with others. Never try to grab *all* the advantages, *all* the profits, all the margins, thereby leaving no room for the other party.

- Making an effort to see things from the other person's perspective. Unless you make a conscious effort to habitually do this, it will be easy to become exceedingly self-cherishing in your interactions with others, and contrary to what you may think, this seriously damages your success potential over the long term. Remember that people have long memories, and goodwill begets goodwill. In the business world you need plenty of goodwill.

- Working with others rather than being a loner. This means building on shared strengths and compensating for weaknesses by pooling diverse capabilities to create a greater whole, so that two plus two does not equal four, but rather five or six or seven.

- Keeping an open mind to new things and new knowledge at all times, allowing for the unexpected to come to your aid. It may be feng shui or it may be some New Age esoteric way of enhancing your chances of success. Whatever it may be, keep your mind open to all that the world may be sending your way.

The development of success attitudes requires belief and commitment. Develop them only after you have thought them through and are convinced of their usefulness. Otherwise you will find it difficult to live with their pervasive presence in your life. The desire to take on a winning posture must come from within you.

A positive attitude helps you win and ensures that you never sabotage yourself. So always endeavour to be as positive as you can. This means being positive in your expectations, in your responses to situations and to people, in your handling of stress, in just about everything. A positive attitude makes you view all things as achievable. It enables you to see the bright side of every bad situation, thereby giving you the strength to keep going. Paint your efforts at building your business in broad strokes of positive vibrations and expectations and everything will become possible. Over time this approach also makes the building process less strenuous and a lot more enjoyable.

MANAGEMENT STRATEGY

Now we can move on to what I always regard as the nitty-gritty of doing business. It has to do with managing your business, managing your staff, managing your problems and managing your money.

To manage, you need to set goals, to plan and to keep track of progress. You need to perform all the key tasks, the routine day-to-day chores, as well as dealing with the crisis situations that crop up with such startling regularity that I have come to regard them as being routine as well. Learning to stay cool is part of becoming a more effective manager.

MANAGING PEOPLE

This has to do with being clear in giving directives, being sure in delegating responsibilities and being sensible in motivating your staff. The best employees are those who thoroughly understand exactly what they have to do. It also helps that they understand the consequences of inefficiencies or inadequacies. As the boss, *you* must communicate these things to your employees as effectively as possible. Bring out the best in them one step at a time. They too need to climb up the learning curve. And do offer praise and encouragement once in a while. From my experience, I have seen a little praise, a little positive acknowledgement go a long way towards motivating people. Genuinely encouraging feedback, articulated in a sincere fashion, also breeds genuine loyalty.

TRACKING THE PROGRESS

This involves a hands-on approach. In the beginning

you will probably have to do everything yourself and this is not such a bad thing. Then you will know the true nature of the processes and problems involved in the running of every aspect of your business. No text book or business school can teach you everything – you learn as you go along. This also keeps you alert and on your toes.

IDENTIFYING THE KEY FACTORS OF SUCCESS

The ability to do this will come naturally if you get really involved in your business. Devote some time each week to just thinking about your working day and how to improve *every* task undertaken – in the selling, the distribution, the marketing, the production process, the administration, the layout of your shop or office, and so on. Focus on one aspect at a time and the important areas will stand out with little effort. Trust your instincts. Trust your own commonsense. And never be afraid to constantly improve the way you handle the various aspects of running your business.

KEEPING ACCOUNTS

You *must* keep accounts. Numbers and accounting can be very boring to many people, but they represent the core of a business in more ways than one. From the start, institute a simple but efficient way of keeping track of the money coming in and going out. It is not necessary to actually know how to put together an income statement or a balance sheet (although, really, it's not at all difficult to learn how), but it is important that you understand what comprise these statements, so you know which numbers are more important than others. Do not allow your mind to develop a mental block to numbers. Make it a part of your daily routine to go through the figures. Eventually, you will know the numbers game inside out.

Set up control-systems (see pages 84–6) to monitor everything that has to do with the movement of money in your business. Thus when you sell something, you receive income and this must be recorded. In the same way, when you buy something for your business, you pay out. This must also be recorded. Everything must be recorded. This is essential to:

- keep track of your business, your cash-flow and your profit
- install safety measures, so you do not get cheated or hoodwinked by either your staff, your suppliers or anyone else you do business with
- enable you, at the end of a period (a month, a quarter or a year) to analyse the profitability or loss of your business. This is vital in assisting you to improve or expand your profitability. More important, it furnishes you with valuable data, which can then be transformed into proper accounting statements to convince bankers and suppliers that yours is a *bona fide* growing business which is professionally run.
- prepare your tax submissions

Once again let me stress that you should not be in any way discouraged if you cannot yet converse fluently in the language of business or balance sheets. What is important is that you know how to run your business in a profitable way. Leave it to the specialists to translate the numbers into financial statements for you, but do keep a record of every single transaction. Set up the systems to do this from the very start.

WATCHING EXPENSES

Monitor the regular weekly and monthly statements. Decide how detailed you wish to be in categorising your expenses. Then analyse the nature of these expenses. Are they within your control? Are they fixed or variable from month to month? Is there wastage? Are they within your budget?

FOCUSING ON COLLECTIONS

This is vital for the business. If you grant credit of any kind, make sure you are keeping an eye out for those who are slow in paying you. Guard against bad debts. A new business cannot afford to have bad debts and most companies have what is known as an ageing account to monitor the length of time taken for debts to be repaid. My advice to new businesses is not to allow credit at all, at least not until you are nicely up on your feet and you know your customers very well indeed.

MANAGING THE MARGINS

This has to do with pricing and profitability. It is the crux of a business. Higher margins mean higher profits, but they also mean higher prices for your products and you could be uncompetitive. Economics students learn about price elasticity – how sensitive your sales are to your price levels. This is something you will have to determine for yourself. It is a judgmental business decision. The management of margins can be extremely vital to the success or failure of your business – and you really must have all the numbers in your head. Be prepared to be flexible, but not to the extent that you totally sacrifice strategic considerations that have to do with consistency.

WATCHING THE BOTTOM LINE

This will follow on from sales, sales margins and expenses. The bottom line is always your profitability, not your cash-flow. Many things affect the bottom line, but the most crucial have to do with:

- the quality of your business decisions – how much to make, how much to buy, how much to stock, how to price your goods, and so forth
- efficiency – how much it costs you to buy or make your product, how well you sell it, how fast you distribute it and the quality of your service

In the course of getting your business on its feet, many things can go wrong and will. The next chapter investigates some common problems of the start-up phase and also explores common risk areas, bottlenecks, cash-flow problems and unexpected difficulties.

Chapter Five

WHEN THINGS GET ROUGH, GET TOUGH

We are constantly told the path to prosperity is one hard climb; that making money is a road strewn with bumps and potholes; that success never comes easy; that it requires sacrifice, determination and resilience; that things almost always go wrong, and sometimes continue going wrong for so long that even the most tenacious of souls are defeated. Is this a fair description? Does the pursuit of wealth cause ulcers, headaches and marriage break-ups? Is it really so difficult? I will have to be honest and say, 'Yes, it's all true.' This is because almost everything that can go wrong in business often does go wrong. But this is also true of life in general. What is important is how you react and respond every time something goes wrong.

The difference between those who *do* make it and those who *don't* is the way they react and respond to difficulties. Successful people tackle their problems without getting into a state of panic or losing their cool. Successful people learn from each daily problem and regard every tough decision as a learning situation. And when things get really rough, the tough get going – facing their sea of troubles, head-on and with calm assurance.

So, what can go wrong? Quite simply, almost everything! Usually, by the time you reach the take-off stage of your new venture, you will have acquired the knack of taking care of daily routine irritations associated with inefficiencies, administrative delays, miscommunications and the like. It is when these minor aggravations take a turn for the worse and threaten the survival of your business that you begin to really feel the pressure. That is when you will be forced to rip away the facade and the gloss and buckle down to making some tough decisions, taking some very firm action.

How can you strengthen yourself from the outset?

How can you stack the dice in your favour and enlarge your chances of surviving major difficulties? The answer lies in *anticipating* what can go wrong. Anticipation is nine-tenths of the battle. Being prepared for all kinds of eventualities is a must.

There are common problems associated with the start-up phase of any business. Below I go through some, which you must be alert to. By keeping an eye out for things that can go wrong from the very start, you will be prepared. This achieves two important results. One, the problem stays small and within your control and two, you will be strong psychologically, because you will have reduced the surprise factor.

Problems Associated with Dishonesty

These take many forms and can be perpetrated against you by your staff, by family members working for you or by a business associate. Skimming (the creation of false expenses), padding of bills, creating false invoices, being supplied sub-standard products, and even direct misappropriation of your funds through cheque frauds and other means are examples.

I cannot list here all the ways a business gets robbed by its associates and staff. What I can tell you is that it goes on all the time, in large and small businesses, which is why corporate entities have internal auditors and sometimes elaborate control systems, which enable managers to spot false figures and false documentation.

The modus operandi of small-time crooks (really there is no other word to describe dishonest people) range from simple acts of doctoring bills and invoices to the more serious one of actually forging your signature on cheques. Don't shake your head in disbelief. I know of many instances when this has happened. In my own corporate career, I have caught staff with their hands in the till, just as I have confronted suppliers who have tried to cheat the companies under my management.

In many instances, one may be tempted to turn a blind-eye to small indiscretions and tolerate minor discrepancies. Just remember that cheats get bolder when they see you being oblivious and allowing them to get away with their dishonesty.

To guard against dishonesty, the best way is to reduce, or better still, completely remove temptation. Do this by:

- establishing proper control-systems of checks and balances from the very start
- personally checking through invoices and payment of bills
- taking your time before entrusting cheque-signing authorisation to others
- undertaking daily supervision of cash coming in (and being banked) and going out

In the early stages of a business, *you* definitely can undertake all of the above. If you start delegating these duties too early, you could be asking for trouble. Trust your employees, but let this translate into total trust only after a period of time. And always check the paperwork and numbers, if not daily, then at least weekly. At the end of each month, set aside time to analyse the books.

If you do come across dishonesty, do not succumb to the temptation of ignoring it because it appears minor. Confront the situation. Warn, firmly and resolutely.

PROBLEMS ASSOCIATED WITH POOR SALES

If you experience problems of this kind in the initial few months, you could be in trouble because poor sales mean income levels are low and your expenses will be eating into your start-up capital.

Paltry sales turnover can be caused by one or a combination of many factors:

- Perhaps you read the market wrong and there really is insufficient demand for your kind of services or your brand of product.
- Your marketing is inadequate. This could be due to poor salesmanship, insufficient promotion, bad distribution, insufficient follow-up on marketing calls, perhaps even a mismatching of marketing strategy and the market itself.
- Your location is a problem.

Whatever the cause of your lack of business, re-analyse your methods and your strategy. I have seen enough 'turnaround' to convince me that when one believes in one's product, a market can always be found or created. Diagnose your problem, identify the bottleneck, stay focused and keep at it.

If you need to incur additional expense for an extra or better salesman or if you need to spend money on promotion, think things through before doing so. Then, having made a decision, implement it with resolution.

If you really do not know what is wrong, get some help. Seek advice from others. Observe what your competitors are doing right. If necessary emulate them, then try to do what has to be done in a more efficient way. But do not copy others blindly. They may have a competitive edge you do not have.

Also, do not give up too soon. Often the early months of a business are the most difficult. Sometimes what you need may be just one big breakthrough. If so, work at it. If after several months, the problem of insufficient sales persists, take a good hard look at the quality of your product. Perhaps there really is something wrong with it. Keep an open mind.

Whatever it is, you must take steps to ensure you are not landed with out-of-date or bad stock. Move it out, at a loss if necessary. At least then you will have recovered part of your inventory cost and protected yourself from incurring further carrying costs. Clear the inventory and start again, making sure you have learnt something from the process.

PROBLEMS ASSOCIATED WITH CASH-FLOW

This is a management euphemism for shortage of cash. When the cash runs out, you are in very serious trouble. You must do something about it urgently. This usually happens if your business is insufficiently capitalised, or if your original projections on income and expenses do not turn out the way you anticipated.

Cash-flow problems take a heavy toll on an entrepreneur's resilience. Above all else, they cause severe worries and often lead to people giving up.

Money problems act like a cancer, eating away at one's confidence. It need not be this way. There is almost always a way out. Do believe me when I tell you that almost every big tycoon I know has had to confront a cash-flow problem at sometime or other.

Re-examine your business. How is it doing? If it is going well, if you are making progress, if the shortage of cash is due to faster growth than anticipated, then you have a good chance of overcoming the problem. You definitely need more capital, or more debt.

Make the effort to raise additional funds. Bring in a partner if necessary. Borrow if necessary. Simultaneously, reorganise your financial arrangements. Speak to your bank. There may be financing options that you haven't yet discovered. In today's business environment, banks and other financial institutions have become quite aggressive in seeking out promising entrepreneurs. Speak to several of them before deciding which of them will be a long-term supporter of your business, because that is the institution to go with. Just like there are fairweather friends, there are also fairweather bankers, who pull the rug from under you at the first sign of trouble. You don't need them.

If your cash-flow problem is created by higher than expected expenses, undertake an honest analysis of each expense. Try to be less extravagant. If you cannot, rework your projections to see whether your projected income levels can be met, and whether your profit margins can be improved to cover the higher expenses. By doing this kind of analysis you will soon get into the habit of monitoring the key financial aspects of your business.

UNEXPECTED PROBLEMS

These are the worst kind. An example would be to discover one morning that you have been operating without a relevant license or a required permit – and to be severely informed of this by one of the regulatory authorities. If this happens to you, do not fret. Go and see the department/statutory body concerned in person and explain your predicament. If you need to pay a fine, do so. Do not lose your cool. Use the opportunity to get to know officers in the relevant department, because they can give you valuable advice.

Unexpected problems also surface when someone sues you. If this happens, don't panic, but do get yourself a good lawyer and do avoid a confrontational stance. Disputes of most kinds can often be settled over a cup of tea, if you take a conciliatory approach instead of allowing a problem to get blown up from a mole hill into a mountain.

When there are changes in legislation, in taxes and tariffs contained in new Budget proposals, these too can cause problems. Even worse is when someone comes out with a new product which makes your product totally obsolete. I know of entrepreneurs in the computer business who stocked up on computer terminals that went out of date almost immediately, and of boutiques carrying brand names which became passé when other new designers came on the scene.

For these reasons, if you are in business, you *must* keep abreast of changes and developments in the economic and corporate environments. Attend seminars and read the trade press, the daily papers and business magazines. Knowledge of change and new developments gives you a wonderful edge and greatly enhances your ability to change course smoothly whenever required.

In the final analysis, coping with growth pains has to do with your ability to sift through nagging trivialities. It helps, if you consciously develop an ability to rise above the petty routine annoyances yet keep an eye out for the more serious problems, which have the potential to develop into crisis situations. Good judgement comes with practice and over time. You will make mistakes along the way – just remember not to be too hard on yourself. Remember also that problems never really go away completely. New ones crop up all the time. The skill of building a business lies in staying stoic and rising above difficulties when things go wrong. And don't be afraid of doing nothing. I have discovered very often that this can be the best solution to a problem you really don't know how to tackle. Let time bring its own solutions.

Chapter Six

STAYING GROUNDED

Having taken the first tentative steps and weathered the early difficult months or years, things will start to go right for you. This is when you will see your sales turnover beginning to grow. The numbers will begin to excite you, because they will be telling you there *is* a demand for your product or service, telling you that you *are* on to a good thing. You could well be the next decade's big success story.

As you enter into this phase of your million-dollar long-term plan and experience some of the fruits of your efforts, you will start to feel the excitement of knowing you are on the right track. But in the pursuit of success, even as you get on a roll, you must also stay solidly grounded.

Of course you should enjoy your success. Success brings a kind of high that really is hard to beat – the high of attainment, when you start to see the promise of glorious things to come. At this stage, it can actually be valuable to take some time out to savour the moment. Let your experience of good results linger in your consciousness for a bit. Savour the high of triumph so that in the future, if and when you feel discouraged or experience less happy times, you will have something solid to draw strength from.

Contemplating your success also allows you to pause and take stock of where you are and where you are heading. Ask yourself, what next?

Exchange ideas with others in a similar position. Absorb new concepts. Explore other people's impressions and strategies. Make contacts and lay the groundwork for establishing a base for future networking. Remember the learning process is a never-ending one. We always have something to learn from others. In your moment of triumph you should not forget this. Those who develop this kind of receptive mind-set are the most likely to sustain their success.

ANALYSING SALES FIGURES

To some of you, the numbers may still just be tentative. To others, they may be gloriously exciting. It is important to understand that for you to conclude that sales really are beginning to take off, an upward trend must be clearly evident. On a graph, the slope must be moving upwards over several months; even better when it is escalating for a whole year!

But before you start jumping for joy, analyse the nature of your sales increases. Are they pushed up because of a special order? Are they sustainable? Was an increase due to some special promotion or marketing strategy? Are you getting more and more repeat orders from satisfied customers?

Understanding the reasons for improved performance is just as important as understanding the reasons for decreases or failures – sometimes more so, because it reinforces your confidence and spurs you on to intensify the positive impact on your business. When you know what it is you are doing right, it is easy to repeat the winning formula.

NEW DIRECTIONS

When sales start to increase, thoughts of expansion and of new directions will begin to entice you. Be very careful. Never let early success cloud your judgement. Guard against impulsive expansions – either in increasing your quantities of stock, in hiring additional staff, in extending your product lines or in opening extra outlets. Continue to crunch the numbers, all the time keeping a close eye on risk/reward ratios, on matching income against additional investment.

This is also the time when you must begin to think strategically (see Chapter 7). Where you are on the learning curve is vital. If you are not yet 100 per cent comfortable with your business, give yourself a couple more months before entertaining thoughts of expansion.

Thinking strategically requires a disciplined analysis, not just of your own business, but also of the competition, the industry you are in and the overall business and trading environment. You must have learnt from all the problems encountered so far. You must examine specific ways of becoming even more efficient, either by raising productivity or by eliminating wasteful practices and reducing unnecessary expenses.

IMPROVING EFFICIENCY

There is always room to improve efficiency. You will have made progress in acquiring the expertise and experience required to run your business. You must now work at profit-enhancement strategies. Do not be too easily satisfied. There is still plenty to be done.

Such an approach – the determined pursuit of excellence – will prepare you well for what comes later, when the numbers get bigger and the size of your operation expands. As you hire more people and get into the realms of strategic decision-making and serious management, the habit of constantly improving will help you make the kind of quantum leaps required to propel you towards the magic six-figure levels.

The entrepreneurial approach of the early days, when your perspective was related to survival strategies, must slowly transform into a more disciplined, organised and management-oriented approach. You will need to delegate and to depend on others. Thus perceptive judgements must come in. Your role will transform from that of an entrepreneur to that of a boss – with all the attendant implications and responsibilities.

DEVELOPING MANAGEMENT SKILLS

You must start to develop practical management skills. At the same time you must continue to think commercially. Your ultimate goal has not changed. All the considerations of the start-up phase – sales turnover, profit margins, cash-flow management, control-systems and the like – continue to be as important as ever. Never forget that in the running of any business, the commercial implications of every decision taken must be carefully weighed.

Important management know-how has to be acquired. This has to do with the way your company and its staff are organised, the way control-systems are implemented, the way you set up channels for regularly monitoring results and the way you design an information system flow within your organisation. As your sales figures increase, you need to ensure that all aspects of information pertaining to your business keep coming to you on a daily basis. This will mean setting up a computerised information system. In recent years, information technology (IT) specialists have become much sought-after professionals. They can make a major difference to the profitability of a company, because the ease with which computers allow access to information within an organisation can massively improve the decision-making process.

INFORMATION SYSTEMS

Information is the basis of all decision making. Unless you are in possession of all the information being generated within your business, you cannot make good or efficient decisions. So how do you set up a good information system in your company?

Start by identifying all the important financial aspects you must monitor on a regular basis. Then set up a system of requiring regular reports from your key staff. Here is a highly simplified checklist of areas that should be monitored:

- sales figures
- stock positions
- collections
- profit margins
- operating and capital expenses

This is only a checklist. It is not exhaustive. Use it to design specific reporting formats for your staff to fill in regularly, to be submitted to you either daily, weekly, fortnightly or monthly.

The information-system flow should expand as you get more familiar with the process and as the things you wish to monitor increase. Make sure all the information you need is flowing up to you and also make certain that you read and analyse this information. Whether you are in business or are employed by a corporation, you must read all management reports and financial statistics regularly. Do not dismiss them as mere paperwork or a waste of time. Accurate and timely information is crucial to the success process.

Hold regular meetings – preferably monthly – to discuss the results of each month's performance with your staff. This is the process of management. It involves discussion, it involves brainstorming and it involves thinking sessions to improve performance for the following month.

At all times keep reports simple and keep meetings short. No trimmings are necessary. But as you expand, reports and meetings will get more complex as more sophisticated analyses become necessary. Reports will have to include ratio analyses, monthly comparisons, reasons for increases/decreases reported and so forth. In these days of computerised information systems, you should not be surprised at the sheer volume of statistics that can be generated (so much that I often wonder how many of the reports spewing forth actually get read). But if you want to stay ahead in the game, either as a business owner or as an operating head of some profit centre, take my advice and do your homework. Always read your management and sales reports.

CONTROL-SYSTEMS

Related to information systems, are a company's control-systems. These are the specific checks and balances which you build into the vulnerable spots of the commercial process of any business. Control-systems have to do with recording transactions, supervising and demarcating areas of authority. For instance, all the buying and selling of the business must be recorded, supervised and properly authorised. All incoming receipts and outgoing expenses have to be itemised and monitored. Control-systems ensure that a company's money – its cash, its receipts and its outgoings – are properly supervised and recorded.

Simple control-systems are easy to set up. Initially this is about making certain more than one person's signature is required to order products or to certify payments, and to make sure one of the signatures required is yours. Other examples are invoices being made out in duplicate or triplicate, with the relevant department heads within your organisation getting a copy and a system for all payment vouchers to be properly authorised by designated staff. These measures safeguard against dishonesty and inefficiency.

Control-systems set the guidelines for the way a company operates. All companies have these guidelines. How elaborate and complicated they are depends on a variety of factors, ranging from the style of management to the nature of the business. Some companies are more relaxed than others, and some bosses are more fussy than others.

You have to decide how strongly you want to control the various aspects of the management function within your company. Control-systems can be very tight and stringent, requiring your approval for every expenditure, or they can be relaxed and laid back – sometimes to the extent that everyone can order anything they like and charge it to the company! Obviously, the ideal is somewhere between these extremes.

COMPUTERS

Computers are essential in the modern business world. When you start thinking seriously about systems and the need for good reports and good control increases, it is always wise to invest in good software programs and use computers to keep track of what goes on. Businesses I know that have invested in good computer systems and software packages from the start have never regretted the investment. They realise that the edge a computer gives them in keeping track of decisions made, of customers' paying profiles, of employee productivity levels and so forth has made a major difference to their success.

A good friend of mine went into the video rental

business. When she started two years ago, she debated whether or not to invest in a computer system to keep track of rentals, customer profiles, stocks, late payments etc. After much thought, she decided in favour of the computer. She has since expanded into three booming outlets. Turnover reached the million dollar level just before she opened her third outlet. When she first started she never expected to grow as fast as she did. She loves her computer and cannot do without it now.

GROWTH

Before we conclude this chapter, let's begin discussing growth.

When you start to grow, let the process be natural. Let growth be demand driven. Stay conservative in the taking of risks; but don't be afraid to take some, especially when you have calculated the sums involved carefully. Budget for growth, but stay lean.

Plough back profits into the business. Continue to

learn from your business associates and widen your circle of business contacts. This is the time when you must create the solid foundation for the second phase of your business, when expansion or diversification becomes a natural strategy. You expand and diversify, not for its own sake, but because it becomes the obvious thing to do.

When you reach this stage, your energies will become focused on strategies of 'how best to proceed' rather than 'should you proceed'. In the next chapter, we shall examine some growth strategies in more depth, spending some time on risk analysis, and also examine the components of strategic positioning and expansion.

Chapter Seven

THINKING STRATEGICALLY

You are now stepping into a different league, where strategic positioning becomes important. Management skills need to be developed and decision-making becomes more complex. At the core of all business success is the real ability to perform better, to deliver better results, to manage better – than your competitors.

To really move ahead, the determined professional or entrepreneur must demonstrate consistently superior performance. No one is judging you. You are judging yourself. Your business may already have reached a comfortable stage, where sales have attained an enviable level, where you have found a comfortable daily routine. But you can do better. You can grow bigger. You can expand.

This is what becoming a millionaire is all about –
having the ambition to step on to the next rung of the
ladder and into a new league. To make the leap you
must start to think strategically.

THE FIVE KEY CONCEPTS

Thinking strategically involves mastering five critical
key concepts:

RESOURCE ALLOCATION

Your cash, your capital, your staff and your contacts -
these are your resources. You must decide on the most
efficient and economical way to maximise their usage
to your advantage.

COMPETITIVE ADVANTAGE

What is it you do better than others? What special
skill, special knowledge, special advantage do you and
your business possess which you can turn to your

advantage, thereby giving you a special edge over your competitors? Thinking this through should enable you to accurately identify who exactly your competitors are. Remember that competitive advantage is about clever and effective market positioning. You can only analyse this properly when you know your business inside out. Positioning is defined in many ways, but they all have to do with your market and the perception of where your products are in that market.

DISTINCTIVE COMPETENCE

What is the one single ability you have which stands out? This may apply to you, your staff or your company as a whole. As a concept it is closely allied to competitive advantage, but a distinctive competence is even more special, as it means something you have which your competitors do not have, or will find great difficulty in acquiring. A distinctive competence is something that is directly relevant to the profitability of your business, and if you can identify it, you will be in a better position to make full use of it. It could be a special skill, an advanced technology or a sharp and resourceful employee – be clear about analysing the strengths or hidden talents within your organisation.

SYNERGY

This is probably the single most important component of strategic thinking (I discuss it in more detail on pages 95–8). What are the areas you can combine, remix, expand or repackage to create higher value and formulate better earning capacity? Examining and identifying the potential for growth through synergistic re-engineering is probably one of the most potent tools of business analysis. The creation of synergy is also one of the better reasons for expansion.

ENVIRONMENTAL ANALYSIS

How do you and your business fit into the larger picture of the industry you are in? Make no mistake – being in business requires you to be alert and sensitive to your operating environment. Those who are not will simply cease to exist.

I had a friend who was extremely successful in

building her business in the late 1980s. She packaged her skills brilliantly and built an extremely profitable PR business. At the height of her success in the early 1990s, she was wooed by countless global agencies. Unfortunately for my friend, she was one of those who seldom read the newspapers or kept up with what was happening in the business and PR world. She was also ignorant of the tremendous importance of making strategic alliances, which could enable her to make the quantum leap to a different league. As a result, competitors quickly overtook her and eventually she lost her competitive advantage. Today her client base has gone down to almost zero and she is winding up her firm.

Thinking through strategic concepts therefore is not just for growth purposes. Often it can also mean the difference between survival and demise. Strategic thinking enables the ambitious entrepreneur to undertake good quality planning. The process is not easy. It cannot be mastered overnight. Believe me, it takes years and a great deal of experience. But you should get started right away! Begin by being familiar and comfortable with the five key concepts mentioned above. Orientate your mind to think in terms of them. Observe. Learn. Take your time. Do not make a desperate attempt to undertake strategic planning immediately. Think first.

Examine each of concept carefully. Analyse it, then relate it to your particular business and circumstances. Every business is unique. It is only after you have undertaken serious appraisal and investigation that you will be able to sift all the information in your mind and collate it in a systematic fashion. Taking this slow and precise approach allows you to define areas in your business that require emphasis and strengthening. Only then can you proceed to identify your strengths and to isolate the 'soft spots'.

Next, identify the processes, products and methods that have brought you success so far. How solid are your perceived strengths? Can they be improved further? Do these strengths give you serious competitive advantage? Could you call all or any of them your distinctive competence – a skill, method or process which really sets you and your company apart from others?

The formulation of strategy, however, does not just involve deep investigation into your strengths and weaknesses. It must also encompass a personal long-term vision. Strategy does not just mean expansion. Strategy actually requires you to rise to the challenges of growth and of change in the environment. It requires the ability and the conviction to carefully identify and then to seize opportunities. And you must also get the timing right.

SYNERGY

Having brought your business to at least a modest level of success, you would have gained considerable knowledge and experience of the business world. You would have identified all sorts of opportunities that represent extensions of your existing business. Here is where synergy comes in. I will stick my neck out and say that the difference between those who *do* make it to the six-figure levels and those who *don't*, is the ability to identify stunning synergies.

Management gurus define synergy obliquely. They will tell you two plus two do not make four, but five or six or even eight! This, they say is synergy. You see the term everywhere, especially in the annual reports of fast-expanding companies. Synergy is such a beautiful term – it can mean so much or it can mean absolutely nothing. It means nothing to a businessperson if it stops at analyses. The ambitious determined entrepreneur or professional explores his or her business for ways, not just to expand, but to operate synergistically and then proceeds to take action. Growth and expansion then become almost natural off-shoots of the business plan. Let me give you a couple of examples of synergy-inspired thinking:

DIVERSIFIED EXPANSION INTO RELATED PRODUCT LINES, WHERE THE DISTRIBUTION OUTLETS ARE THE SAME AS YOUR EXISTING ONES

This kind of expansion is what the experts call building a 'critical mass', that is creating the volume of business which enables you to enjoy synergistic advantages arising from economies of scale in distribution. In other words, while your volume of business increases, your average cost of distributing (or selling) per unit goes down, thereby enlarging your overall profit margin. Looked at another way, the marginal cost of expansion to you is thus lower than when you first started. This is one of the most compelling reasons for expansion.

DIVERSIFIED EXPANSION INTO RELATED PRODUCT LINES, WHERE THE SOURCE OF SUPPLY IS THE SAME

The line of reasoning is similiar to the above, but this time the synergistic advantage occurs on the supply side. In some businesses, competitive sourcing is a crucial component of success. If your business falls into this category, look for synergy in this area.

BUYING OR MERGING WITH ANOTHER BUSINESS, THAT IS SIMILIAR TO OR RELATED TO YOURS

Synergy crystallises when you realise two similar businesses under one management can lead to profits equivalent to perhaps three or more, managed and operated separately.

It is often said that managing one outlet and managing ten outlets selling the same kind of product or service, requires the same amount of effort and energy. In academic jargon, this introduces the concept of marginal costs. We know that many of the processes and job functions that are involved in the running of businesses can easily be centralised under a single management. In fact, this organisational approach has been the core principle for many of the successful franchise businesses that we see flourishing today.

Look at Kentucky Fried Chicken and McDonald's. Each of these chains have honed their business strategy to such a fine art that opening new outlets is a breeze. They already have the know-how, all the expertise required, available at their fingertips, so that the only critical decisions are where to site the next outlet and how to pull the customers in. Companies like these rise or fall on the excellence of their distinctive competence.

MAKING THE QUANTUM LEAP

Once you get used to thinking strategically, you will be amazed at the thousands of ideas and new opportunities you suddenly become aware of. It is at this stage that you will begin to view the commercial world from a different perspective. Mentally, you will start to take notes, start to tuck in bits and pieces of information you pick up in conversations with suppliers and salesmen. You will automatically analyse how new developments within your commercial environment affect your business.

You will become very conscious of costs and margins. You will start to tell yourself, 'Hey I can do this better,' or 'I can supply this at a lower cost.' In short, your planning antennae will have become sharpened to spot and recognise so called 'imperfections in the marketplace', which you can take advantage of. When you notice these subtle changes in yourself, you are ready to make the quantum leap.

You will begin to see the real synergies that come your way. When you do, resist the urge to plunge in without first undertaking some basic business planning and some risk analysis. These are tedious adjuncts to the management process at this stage of your business development, but they cannot be ignored. You may feel your instincts are good enough. And you may be right. You may even be very lucky. But unless you develop the right habits from the beginning, you could be setting yourself up for larger failures later on.

Gone are the days when an entrepreneur could manage a growing business in the old-fashioned haphazard way, when numbers were calculated on the back of an envelope and decisions made on the basis of 'gut feeling' alone. Today's business environment is extremely sophisticated, well-informed and fast-changing. Competition is very much keener. Capital is more freely available, so new businesses are being set up all the time to compete against you. Markets are also getting more perfect and customers are getting smarter.

Even companies that enjoy advantages due to some special franchise, contact, competence or information cannot hope to have the advantage for very long. No one really has a monopoly of information or expertise any more. The world has become very competitive. Thus, the person who gets ahead is the one who can spot opportunities, undertake analyses and then take the calculated risks quicker than anybody else.

The corollary of this is that, today, opportunities are available to more people to really make it big. If you are genuinely determined to move into the millionaire league, you must understand this. The world's business environment seems to be very conducive to an entrepreneurial explosion. If your business is currently at a real take-off stage, start thinking strategically. Be ambitious.

In the next chapter, I shall explore one special area of growth – through acquisition and merger. No, this is not a strategy open only to public companies or big tycoons. You too can grow via acquisition. You too can package meaningful and strategic alliances. We shall investigate the various methods of valuing a business, and we shall examine some of the techniques of successful negotiation.

Chapter Eight

BUYING A BUSINESS

For some, buying a business is a way of getting started. For others, growth by acquisition is an option that can make strategic sense. Buying a business can also be a means of diversifying, or of expanding and integrating operations. If this is an option you wish to consider, it is useful to know the basics of valuing a business. This gives you solid fundamentals with which to formulate your negotiating strategy.

GETTING STARTED

When I decided to leave the security of corporate employment to venture into my own business, I took a short cut and made a quantum leap. I identified the kind of business I wanted to try my hand at, persuaded some big-name partners to come in with me, arranged the financing and made a bid for a company I had 'discovered'.

When I first spotted it – by casually flicking through an auditors' report of the company while visiting an investment banker friend of mine – Dragon Seed Co Ltd was at a stage in its evolution when it sorely needed some real glamour and, indeed, was crying out for a new owner. For years it had been a favourite of rich Hong Kong *tais tais* (wives), but now it was suffering from neglect and ill-will between the families of its three controlling shareholders. This chain of department stores and retail outlets, which had its own building in Queens Road Central, Hong Kong (a very prime piece of real estate), had had an excellent reputation – except that the company had also grown sleepy and rundown and looked very tired indeed.

I found the company in late October and by the beginning of January of the following year, I had successfully acquired it and had myself installed as a significant shareholder. By being very focused and determined, I became the Executive Chairman of my very own department store group. As it turned out, it was the perfect acquisition for me (and my partners). Why? Because we knew exactly why we were buying the company and we also knew exactly what we were going to do with it.

You too can leapfrog into the commercial business world by buying into a company. It can be a wonderful way of getting started, especially if the business has been around for some time. Any established company is bound to have a wealth of business contacts and associates, and these alone should be worth a great deal in terms of goodwill. If you feel you have the ability to inject profitable new ideas and activities into a company's under-utilised resources, it could be a splendid way of getting started in business. In other words, if you can find a company that is under-performing in terms of profits or only just keeping up with the times, and you are convinced you can do a better job, you should go for it.

Financing can be tricky but it is not an insurmountable problem for those of you who, like me, have a successful work-record covering many years. Better still is having some expertise in the packaging of capital. And, yes, the acquisition route is an option only really open to those of you who do have some capital, or have access to it. But acquisition of a small- or medium-sized company should be within reach of many of you.

GROWTH BY ACQUISITION

Growth by acquisition is a great way of expanding your business. In the last chapter, I wrote at some length about synergy, and said that one of the most effective methods of enlarging your business was to be on the lookout for other businesses that have a synergistic fit with yours. Rather than having to go through the process of starting from scratch all over again, you can pay a premium to acquire a ready-made organisation that offers the potential of smoothly merging with yours. In many instances, if you have done your homework, the resulting advantages arising from economies of scale alone can be very real.

Using this kind of strategy to expand is highly popular with publicly listed corporations, mainly because the financial system allows such companies to create (issue) new shares as payment for any business being acquired. To make things even more convenient, merchant banks and stockbroking firms can also underwrite these newly-created shares (underwriting means guaranteeing to buy at a certain price).

Private limited companies can also grow by acquisition, but their ability to use this method of financing is limited, mainly because the shares of their company, being private and not listed on any exchange, have no ready market. This is one of the most compelling reasons why companies decide to go for listing. It expands their options for getting extra financing, should they wish to expand. Stated another way, public listing of its share equity allows a company to grow much faster than if that equity had stayed in private hands.

Notwithstanding this, however, private limited

companies can certainly offer an exchange of shares, if both parties agree to the deal. Or you may be able to find a partner who is prepared to buy any new shares issued, so that the end result is that your company's capital is enlarged. Naturally your percentage holding goes down, because you now have a new partner, and the person who sold you his company has received cash in payment.

There is, of course, nothing stopping you from using cash to buy a company, and this is probably the most common method of doing so. Usually this cash represents a combination of internally generated funds – retained profits from the company or additional capital put up by you – and bank borrowings. Yes, banks do consider giving acquisition financing, especially if you have a track record and you are able to demonstrate that you have the expertise and the experience to successfully manage the acquisition. Usually the shares of the acquired company can be used as collateral for such financing.

Besides, it is always useful to obtain the opinion of professional bankers, since they usually run through the key financial aspects involved with a certain level of professionalism and may be able to spot things about the intended acquisition that you may have missed.

QUALITATIVE AND QUANTITATIVE ANALYSIS

Assessing the ways in which another business might fit in with yours is referred to as the *qualitative* part of your analysis. Much of the reasoning involved is commonsense, based on your knowledge of the industry or business you are in.

Usually, by the time you reach a stage when growth by acquisition becomes a serious option, you will already be in a position to gauge, almost instinctively, any advantages of acquiring the additional outlets, branches, product lines, distribution system or marketing capability, belonging to the company you are eyeing. Part of the qualitative analysis involves having a plan for post-acquisition management. It is not clever to buy a company which seems to have a nice fit with your existing business if you don't really know how to implement the actions required to take advantage of the fit.

Do not ever fall for nice-sounding jargon. Always take a very practical approach. Look for real strengths which complement your own. These could be profitability, ownership of a great location, branch offices in geographical areas in which you are not yet represented or some superior system or process which will enhance your own – the perceived advantage can take many different permutations. Thinking through the reasons for acquisition is always a very useful exercise in itself, because whether you end up actually making the acquisition or not, you would almost always benefit your own business by making the analysis.

In addition to this commonsense approach, it is necessary to also do the relevant calculations and examine the financial aspects – the balance sheets and the profit and loss statements. Basic calculations of net worth and profitability must be made, and all liabilities thoroughly investigated. This is the *quantitative* part of the analysis, and if accounting is not your forte, it is worthwhile employing a reputable firm of accountants to undertake what is called a 'due diligence' analysis and investigation.

On the business side, it is seldom difficult to make forecasts of merged sales, expenses, margins and profits, plus any anticipated savings in expenses, if you know your business well enough. Just be careful not to be unrealistically optimistic when going through your own projections.

Remember that having to deal with a different team of employees, who may or may not be resentful of new owners, can often be a veritable minefield. Acquisition management is dotted with unexpected potholes and problems – the solutions to which can be so expensive as to undermine any strategic gain arising from the acquisition. Indeed, post-acquisition management is never easy. Look out for companies that have powerful trade unions or militant employees – they can be a nightmare!

Indeed people management is often the most difficult aspect of post-acquisition management – and the larger the company you are buying the more difficult the problems of people management can be. So do your homework. It doesn't hurt to talk to some of the middle-level employees to gauge their responses to a possible takeover.

EVALUATING A BUSINESS

Putting a price on a business is a very subjective exercise. Yes, there are specific methods of valuation, and any number of professional firms will be only too happy to lend their expertise in this area. Let me list here some of the more commonly accepted methods of valuation – those used by accountants, banks and financiers:

PRICE-EARNING (PE) MULTIPLE METHOD

Here the profit after tax is multiplied by say a number between eight and ten. Thus if the profit of the company is $230,000, the value of the company based on a multiple of ten will be $2.3 million. If you use this method, check which year's profits you are using, whether it is last year's *actual* profit or next year's *forecast* profit.

Also, check the multiple being used. Is it the accepted 'norm' for your industry? A useful guide is the stock market price of companies that make similar products or are engaged in the same industry. Check the average price-earning multiple of their stock prices and then make some discount adjustments for the non-listed status of the company you are acquiring.

THE NET-ASSET VALUE (NAV) METHOD

Here, the company's net assets are calculated, then adjusted for market valuations of its fixed assets, like land and buildings. This method is often used for asset-rich companies, such as property development companies. Remember that the word 'net' means you must deduct all liabilities. If after the deduction, you get a negative figure, it means that the company is technically insolvent. This does not mean that the company is not worth buying. Sometimes this can be an opportunity of acquiring something cheap, especially if you know you have the ability to 'enhance' the value of the assets. An example of this is where there is undeveloped or agricultural land on the books, which may, over time, be enhanced if you can succeed in getting the land-use converted to something more lucrative.

PERMUTATIONS AND COMBINATIONS OF THE ABOVE TWO METHODS

Sometimes a company is valued by adding the net-asset value with the price-earning value (for example, the net-asset value plus five times the profit after tax). Or it can even be calculated as a multiple of the net-asset value itself (for example, as twice the net-asset value).

Implicit in all calculations of value will be some value placed on 'goodwill'. Do not be frightened off by this example of an intangible asset. Goodwill does have real value and sometimes this may be just the name of the company. For instance, if the name is a well-known brand name, with a good reputation built up over several years, surely some value can be placed on it, especially if it has high-recognition status?

It is very important to be at least familiar with some of the valuation methods mentioned above, because knowing about these methods can help you enormously in the negotiating process. You cannot negotiate effectively unless you know the basis of how a business is priced. But negotiations are never about price alone. Usually the astute businessman or woman will also throw in required guaranties and warranties to ensure that certain safeguards are put in place. And finally, the terms of payment are also a negotiating point. You should discuss the payment period, the interest rates payable (if any) and perhaps payment via a combination of paper (shares) and cash.

Do study some of the deals made by the public companies, that are covered in the daily business papers. Try to understand them. Learn from some of the more creative strategies of financing, acquisition and diversification. Not all of them are clever of course, but reading about them makes you think.

In the next chapter, we shall take the opposite perspective and look at the important factors to consider should you decide to sell your business, and the reasons for doing so.

Chapter Nine

SELLING A BUSINESS

Into everyone's life come many opportunities, and seizing them will create significant milestones and crossroads that shape the future. Decisions made at these crucial turning-points can drastically alter your lifestyle and career path.

As someone who is halfway to achieving your goal of making your first million, you will find yourself being faced with choices. Once you succeed in developing a business, you will find that at some stage you will have to confront the difficult decision of whether to cash in your investment – sell out, take the profits and turn your back on the business world. It may not be something you even want to think about – many look on the business they build as they would a baby. It is not difficult to get emotionally attached to a business, which can come to represent so much of you.

I have never formed an attachment to any of my jobs or businesses. I have always viewed them as the means to an end – the end, being to attain a level of financial independence that would allow me to be my own person. I realised very early in my life that unless I was independently rich, I would not have the freedom to pursue the kind of lifestyle I wanted. This was a fundamental truth that spurred me on, creating my intense desire to make enough money to retire completely from the corporate world.

I used all the skills and resources that I had been blessed with. This meant not only applying whatever management and business skills I had gained through my work experience, but also, and I think more significantly, all the feng shui knowledge I had gathered together over the years. I think that the decision to make myself into a real and meaningful millionaire coincided exactly with the time when I decided to use feng shui. To do this, I bought a new apartment on the Peak in Hong Kong and had the entire place made over according to feng shui principles. So for me, when the time came to sell out and take the profits, by selling the business I had turned around, I did. I persuaded my financiers and partners to do the same. Together we sold the Dragon Seed Company after eighteen months of ownership.

Having said all of the above, I also have to say that I really can understand how others might not want to sell out but, instead might wish to take the business they have nurtured on to greater heights. As I stated earlier, it is you who must decide the magnitude of your own ambition and the direction you want your working life to take. You are the one in control.

WHY ARE YOU SELLING?

Those of you who might want to toy with the idea of selling out should approach the project with the same kind of diligence that you put into building up the business in the first place. The key to getting good value for what you have spent your time creating is to clarify very carefully in your mind why you wish to sell. Here are some possible reasons:

- You sell to cash in your profits, so you can make other investments. You are one of those who believe that 'a bird in the hand is worth two in the bush'. Besides, you also believe that the economy could slow down. You don't want to risk a business downturn. You want to sell out while values are still high. Here it is a situation of being clever about the timing.

- You sell so you can stop working, to look after other areas of your life. Perhaps your children are growing up faster than you realised. They need you. Perhaps your husband needs you – his career is taking off. He's making more money now and you would prefer to be fully supportive of him. Besides, you have got it out of your system – you have proved to yourself that you can do it. You can now lead a more family-centred life, more confident and self-assured than ever.

- You sell because you don't want the headaches of running the business anymore. It's no longer fun having to get up early day after day, go to the office, work eighteen hours, then return home and continue to worry about the business. The early enthusiasm has faded along with the daily grind, the never-ending problems and the decisions which have to be made. In short you have succumbed to executive stress. You just want out. Money has not lost its appeal, but the glitter has faded somewhat.

- You sell because you feel that you can't take the business any further, that it has reached its limits under your management. Why? Because you do not want to grow any bigger, and yet you know that if you don't, you are going to lose out to your competitors. Far better, then, to sell out and let someone else take the business you built further.

  Perhaps you will retain a small stake in the business and let someone else enhance its value for you. From being an entrepreneur manager you then become an investor.

- You sell because the business is not doing as well as you had hoped. Profits are falling and the thought of having to turn it all around is both tiresome and daunting. You can see the writing on the wall. Things really are not as good as the figures appear to demonstrate. How do you know? You know because you've been in the business long enough. You can see that companies such as yours must diversify, change direction, to survive. And you are too tired to start afresh. Far better to sell the business now while the accounts still look good.

- You sell simply because you cannot resist an offer you have been made. Well-run entrepreneurial businesses, which demonstrate solid potential for take-off, are great favourites with expansion-minded tycoons and large corporations, who are always on the lookout for such successful enterprises.

Usually their offers are hard to resist because they often come very nicely packaged. The offer is often not merely a lump-sum payment for the business, which allows you to enjoy some immediate profits, but frequently a lucrative management contract is thrown in. This gives you the option of staying on to continue running the business, retain a small stake and enjoy the umbrella of a large company's contacts, power and influence.

This type of offer is perfect for the man or woman who has not lost sight of his or her goal of making it to the seven- or eight-figure level. It is perfect for anyone who wants to continue on the climb upwards, and often represents the opportunity of making a super quantum leap to pursue big dreams. Why? Because being bought over by a bigger company often means instant access to fresh new capital.

It is this type of offer that spells recognition of capabilities, an acknowledgement of hard work. It opens up exciting fresh avenues for further growth, because in this kind of sell-out, the potential exists for still better things to come. It is another wonderful way of making the major leap into boardrooms of substance. And yes, it can happen to you or to anyone who is determined enough to make it happen.

If this last scenario appeals to you, mould your business so that it becomes attractive to the big corporate players. Take the strategic approach. Look for synergies, both for you and a potential 'predator'. Identify possible buyers. You can wait for them to find you, target you for takeover. But you can also be pro-active and take the initiative.

FINDING A BUYER

Your chances of success in finding a buyer yourself are

about fifty/fifty, and, contrary to conventional advice, and practice, I have found that actively looking for a buyer does not necessarily decrease the value of one's business. Very much depends on how the packaging is done. I refer to the packaging of the company as well as the packaging of yourself. As long as you are clever about the sale and not desperate to cut a deal too quickly, as long as your business is sound and has solid growth potential, there is no reason why an active campaign to find the right buyer will not succeed.

If you are in the market for a buyer, be prepared. Have your fixed assets, like land and buildings, valued beforehand, so that these figures are immediately available. Such valuations should be undertaken by a reputable valuer (and should also be up-to-date). Next, make certain that a reputable firm of auditors has always properly audited your accounts. Finally, make certain that your business is 'squeaky clean', with a healthy balance sheet, good creditors and debtors, solid reputable suppliers and customers and reputable bankers. You should work actively towards having such attributes from the very start of a business, so that its 'goodwill' value is considerably enhanced. You will then be in a good position to expect a premium to be attached to the price tag of your company.

When you have found a buyer, be very understated in your negotiating strategy. Let the buyer package the deal for you. This is particularly important if the buyer is a much larger company than yours. Be open to the price range suggested when negotiating; be willing to listen when the payment package is suggested. Do not give an immediate response. Just do a great deal of listening and then sleep on specific offers made.

Before entering into negotiations, you should have already firmed up an acceptable price for your company in your mind. Do not think in terms of a single price. Work around a price range – the highest and the lowest prices you would be prepared to accept, depending on the attraction of the entire package.

Be very clear about what you are getting and what you are giving. If you wish to still have a role in running the business, make this one of the terms of sale. Package it as a merger of sorts. But remember, even as you frame the conditions under which you give up total control of your business, when you accept such a deal, no matter what kind of safeguards you factor into the agreement, you are no longer the sole boss. You may still wield considerable influence, but you do not have the kind of authority you had before, because you have sold out the controlling interest in the company.

This kind of sell-out, therefore, has considerable pros and cons. If this is the option you have decided upon, there is no room for emotion, or regrets. Ask yourself if you can work under remote centralised control-systems, if you can take orders from cold unsympathetic bureaucrats, who have no idea how your business was run but who now insist that you follow company policy. Get used to the idea of making formal presentations for approval to spend the company's money. Get used to working within the corporate culture of the new owner. Allow time and effort to make the adjustments needed. There is a price to pay, but it could be very worthwhile.

Overall, do think things through carefully before deciding to sell. If upon reflection, selling does not seem to be the ideal way of proceeding, you can also examine other strategies for expansion, other exciting ways of raising capital. We shall examine these in the next chapter.

Chapter Ten

CREATING WEALTH

In the last two chapters, we toyed with the idea of buying a business and then flirted with the idea of selling a business. These are two major strategic options available to anyone wishing to make money in the business world and they are not necessarily mutually exclusive.

Corporate strategic directions often encompass both options into their medium- and long-term plans – selling portions of their businesses while expanding into other directions. These other directions may be taking the company towards more specialised areas or into special marketing niches, or they may represent diversification moves. In the business of making money, believe me, any and every direction has the potential to take you to the very top. The key success factor is not the direction you take, but the commitment and energy you put into getting wherever you decide to go.

DEVELOPING A STRATEGY FOR GROWTH

Directions of growth and development are often complex and require strategic thinking (see Chapter 7). It is you who undertakes this thinking. If you have made an implicit decision to grow your business and want to move into a bigger league, it is vital that you start to think a little deeper.

Consider now the more important strategic issue of how you can go about creating value through growth and expansion. The creation of value creates wealth. Creating value involves determining your medium- and long-term intentions. Thinking this through gives you, and your staff, a sense of direction and provides a basis for defining future targets, identifying critical success factors and designing meaningful performance measures.

The long-term view also encourages you to separate transient issues from strategic ones, so that the building process becomes more coherent within the framework of defined goals. This then leads to the kind of cohesive approach required to maintain past successes and to build on what has been achieved so far – thereby creating value because you can maintain, and indeed enhance, your profits. Thus creating value has to do with ends and means. As an end, it describes the vision of value desired and as the means, it lays out ideas and actions required to make the vision a reality.

Creating value in any business should always involve looking at several important issues that appear to be superficially conflicting, requiring trade-offs to be made. Look at some examples:

- immediate concerns versus long-term concerns
- the company-wide level versus the business unit or departmental level
- accounting for now versus accounting for later
- playing it safe versus taking risks

If you start thinking through the nature of your business decisions, you will be able to generate additional trade-offs that appear to pit short-term profits against long-term value. This is especially true when your business is already successful, and you are trying to decide where to go from there. The strategic approach allows you to clarify your thoughts in a productive and constructive way.

You know you must analyse your business thoroughly if you wish to formulate clear and strategic directions. To ensure that you do this as thoroughly as possible, let me repeat the five key concepts of strategic analysis (see also Chapter 7):

- identifying your distinctive competence
- knowing where you have the competitive edge
- creating synergy
- clever environmental monitoring (internal and external)
- optimising resource allocations (capital, manpower etc.)

An analysis based on these concepts will enable you to

design the major ingredients of your business *and* to develop a clear corporate strategy. It will clarify your vision, separating what is deemed achievable from what is not. From this you should then be able to formulate a strategic blueprint which will 'add to' the value of your business. Do not make the mistake of thinking that only big corporations benefit from this kind of strategic thinking and analysis. Remember that no business is ever too small to benefit from having a clever strategy; and don't forget the value of your business has to do with growth, consistency of growth and sustainability of growth. Plan to have this reality factored into the strategic direction for the future of your company and you will have created real wealth.

So if you want to become a millionaire and to eventually become seriously wealthy (as opposed to being merely rich), you must work hard at creating value. How can you do this? Here is a quick checklist (which is by no means exhaustive) of the questions to ask yourself to stimulate further thinking on how you can enhance the value of your company.

- **On the big picture facing you,** how can overall long-term profit increases be maintained and even enhanced? How can the company's product(s) be developed further? How can the company's markets and market share be enlarged? What are the growth options facing the company? Are there interesting areas for diversification? Are there promising areas for internal expansion? Are there businesses for sale which create synergistic advantages? Should the company disinvest certain product lines?

- **On the selling and packaging** side of the business, which of your market segments can be enlarged? Can your marketing mix – publicity, advertisement, imaging etc. be improved? Can new markets (new places to sell to) be developed? Can the promotion strategy be improved, enhanced, or dropped? Should the price/profit margin relationship be reviewed? Should distribution outlets be expanded or contracted? Can the sales force be made more productive?

- **On production** is there any new technology you should be looking at? Can your productivity be increased? Is there unutilised capacity? Are there better, more productive processes to use? Is your quality the best you can achieve?

- **On your people strength**, is the employer/

employee relationship conducive to growth? Should the management structure be reorganised? Is there under utilisation of manpower? Will future expansion require large investments in additional staff? Is additional training of the staff required to motivate and raise productivity?

- **On the money side**, do you have a proper long-term finance strategy (on raising new capital for growth)? Are the control-systems that are in place capable of coping with growth? Are banking relationships conducive to growth? Is the accounting policy conducive to enhancing the value of the company?

OTHER APPROACHES

So far, what I have done is to offer one small theoretical model for analysis – the five key concepts approach, with some helpful questions thrown in. While this is useful, you should also proceed from here to investigate other models and other approaches, paying particular attention to the finance, and accounting functions.

In fact, as you grow and become bigger, your status

in your commercial and business environment will probably make this little book inadequate. But by then this book should have done for you what I am hoping it will do – spur you on to great and greater success. You could seek out bigger and more specialised books. But I doubt that any of them can offer full-formed ideas and solutions. I have discovered that most management and business books are often dogmatic and usually very theoretical. Real life is seldom so rigidly focused that any single book, theory, concept or planning model can take care of all the variables confronting you.

When I am in doubt and feel inadequate to undertake any serious strategic thinking, I have found that the most reliable person to turn to for help and encouragement is myself – actually, what I term my higher self, the self who resides deep inside me, who knows a lot more than my surface self realises. This higher self has deeply developed instincts that are based on the sum total of all my experiences and remembers things and lessons which my surface self has long forgotten. It is the same for you and everyone else. So when I need guidance, I usually relax, switch my mind to fun things and allow the answers to surface gently. Some people call this alpha-level mediation. Others call it creative visualising for solutions. I call it allowing the higher self to surface. If you explain to yourself what the creation of wealth is and state that you really want it, your higher self will help you work towards it.

MANAGING THE UNEXPECTED

It is usually not possible for anyone to undertake a functional analysis along the lines suggested without allowing for any number of things to go wrong. For example, your figures could be unreliable or they could simply be unavailable, forcing you to make estimates that could be inaccurate. Or perhaps a key member of staff, on whom you relied heavily, has decided to leave you, thereby forcing you to re-evaluate your chances of success. Or your assumptions could be wrong – and so on.

Many millionaire entrepreneurs will tell you that strategy re-orientations or strategic expansions do not just 'happen', simply as a result of a decision to do so. Rather, the character of expansion is such that it takes place in a series of brief and sometimes unexpected quantum leaps. Some of these leaps may have been forced on you by the pressure of external developments. For instance, the loss of a major customer could well force you to change your marketing strategy. A new opportunity or a new location could make you re-evaluate your situation. Thus changes of direction can emerge as responses to an evolving situation.

Notwithstanding this, defining a long-term plan and targeting for a certain growth rate does ensure an awareness of business realities, that can help you rise to meet the challenges of new competitive pressures and new opportunities. Unless you are poised mentally to meet these challenges, it is likely that when unexpected developments threaten your company's health, you will not be adequately prepared and could well lose out. This could mean a potential 'loss of value'.

THINKING AHEAD

Successful entrepreneurs seldom sit on their laurels. In the same way that corporate giants undertake continious corporate planning and adopt value enhancement strategies to their operating decisions, you too must realise that the business that thrives is the one that has value, and such a business is one that grows, not one that stays static. And growth, whatever the circumstances, should always result from careful strategic thinking.

This is not always fully appreciated by inexperienced observers of the corporate scene. Stock analysts, for instance, especially impressively qualified young analysts who have wonderful theoretical knowledge and expertise but who lack experience of the operational environment, seldom realise that successful tycoons, who appear to make snap decisions or take enormous financial risks, do so only after they have weighed the risks thoroughly.

They know the tremendous importance of creating value and they understand that sometimes, in order to protect future profits or sustain growth rates, it is necessary to sacrifice immediate profits. I have observed many 'self-made men', making instant decisions that have far reaching consequences on the strategic direction of their companies. Often, while these decisions may appear to be 'instant', the truth of the matter is that they seldom are. Prior to the decision to acquire a company – to buy a second-hand plant that suddenly becomes available, to diversify into a totally unrelated business, to put down the payment on an enormous piece of real estate – has usually gone a great deal of thought. These types of chief executive know their business and their strengths inside out. They are very clear about their ultimate goals.

AIMING HIGH

Once set on the path of creating value, experienced successful entrepreneurs seldom waver. We can learn crucial lessons from people like that. What stands out most, from my many years of observing such people, is their almost obsessive determination to achieve their goals. It is often scary to watch, especially at close quarters – the way they take risks, believing so much in themselves, their abilities and their vision, that they risk losing all they have achieved – to make that huge leap into a different league.

Even the lack of immediately available funds to fuel their ambitions rarely stop them. To raise the required capital, some of them have used their successful business as collateral to take on huge debts. These people bank on their confidence to succeed. When it comes to building a business – the million-dollar type of business – these people know that it is not just the year-to-year profits they are after, it is the promise of increasing profits and the consistency of profits growth and the expectation of this consistency bringing them the 'creation of value' that they desire. It is this creation of value that propels them to become multi-millionaires and even billionaires.

This then should be the ultimate goal of the entrepreneur who wants to make it into that magic millionaire/billionaire circle. Strategic formulation of a goal plan is what will open up the opportunities that your successful small or medium-sized business throws at you. If you already own such a business, and it is doing well, go for it!

FUNDING FOR GROWTH

If what is keeping you from taking a major step forward is lack of capital, one way to proceed is to bring in partners who have the money and can see the upside potential of value creation in your company. Sell them a slice of the action. But do not go into partnership with individuals. Look for the big-time corporation who can multiply your value a hundred times over!

But be aware that if you opt for this route, you could lose control of your company. You might have to dilute your stake to raise fresh capital. So you will have to decide whether to limit any new equity placed in other people's hands to 49 per cent. Remember that when you bring in partners this way, you can price your business as a multiple of your latest profits (see pages 111–2). Thus partners brought in after you have become successful in building your business, should expect to pay a premium to join forces with you.

The money of course does not go into the company – it goes to you, because the transaction involves you selling out. This way you will have a smaller stake in a company that stays the same size.

Another way of raising money for expansion is to 'issue new shares' in your company – up to say 49 per cent of the enlarged equity to your new partner or partners. If you do it this way, the money flows into the company and you will have a smaller stake in a bigger company. After enlarging the capital of the company by bringing in additional shareholders, you can then proceed to arrange bank facilities. Banks are usually very amenable to lending money to companies that are strongly capitalised and showing a healthy stream of earnings.

In the next chapter, we shall assume that you have opted for ambitious expansion – the quantum leap which has taken you beyond the million-dollar level in terms of profits and probably several millions in terms of sales. Your company is no longer just one company – you probably have subsidiaries as well. And you have the nucleus of a management team to help you manage growth and change.

Chapter Eleven

Managing Change

One of the often disputed realities about wealth creation is that it is easier to make money than to keep on making it. Put another way, once you have made your first million, contrary to popular belief, making further millions can get more difficult. I have often wondered about this and have come to the conclusion that the average entrepreneur, having succeeded, is often reluctant to change his or her success formula. Moreover, this is frequently coupled with a reluctance to take any more risks.

It is now a case of having something real and tangible to lose, as opposed to the early days when risk-taking was easier – the stakes were not so high then. There is also, of course, the instinctive conviction that having tasted the fruits and trimmings of wealth, one should cling desperately to the well-trodden and proven successful path. One becomes more averse to taking the inherent risks involved in making any kind of change – sometimes to the extent of becoming quite dogmatic in one's attitudes. It is like having a mental block.

Alas, the world of business and commerce is never static. Today, with the breathtaking speed of new developments, new technologies, new competitors and new angles being introduced into the market place, anyone who blinds himself or herself to new developments stands in serious danger of becoming a casualty of just such environmental and macro-economic changes.

Part of an on-going wealth-creation formula involves accepting the fact that every business organisation must view itself as being perpetually in a state of change. We have noted that to survive and thrive, businesses, professionals and people must grow. There must be innovation – the development of new products, the expansion into new markets, the introduction of new technology and the improvement of work methods and practices. Such innovation or change seldom 'just happens'. You, as the one in control of your own destiny, as your own boss and the owner of your business, must be the one to initiate, plan, execute and implement such changes. Which is what is meant when management gurus talk about the need for leadership, and for vision.

NEW HORIZONS

One of the most outstanding management books of the past decade must be *The Change Masters*, a breakthrough book written by one of the leading professors of the Harvard Business School – Professor Rossabeth Moss Kanter. The views and theories expounded in this best-selling book were based on years of intensive research into businesses at various stages of their life-cycles. Professor Moss Kanter says:

. . . no lasting achievement is possible without a

vision and no dream can become real without action and responsibility. The years ahead should be a good time for dreamers and visionaries of the business world, for the barriers to innovation, the roadblocks to inspiration and imagination are being knocked down, one by one . . . for example physical space is no longer a barrier to consummating any deal anywhere; the speed of information transmission, has extended the reach of business to every corner of the globe, and small businesses can now do more of the things only larger ones could do in the past due to computer power at vastly lower costs. . ..

Worldwide, countries are lowering barriers to enterprise by privatising public corporations, allowing freeflow of commerce across borders, deregulating industries and, most of all, encouraging entrepreneurship. For today's individuals, barriers to ambition are progressively being demolished. Even within organisations, weakening hierarchies and broader participation in problem-solving and decision-making have now placed senior corporate positions, that come with equity offerings, within reach of every ambitious and productive individual – no matter where on the corporate ladder he or she presently stands.

Company heads and business leaders now recognise that the future is for those who embrace the expanding horizons, those who find new solutions that permit you to do more with less, those who play the business game according to the new rules. To move on from where you are, therefore, you must have vision.

When vision is lacking, competitive constraints will force you to react to virgin scenarios. Change is inevitable and this realisation has led many to observe that the only thing that remains constant is the need to change. Recognising the need to change is so vital that sometimes even the largest and strongest corporations can be destroyed or seriously injured if their chief executives are unprepared for, or are dogmatically resistant to change.

IMPLEMENTING CHANGE

Change is often resisted by those with a stubborn mind-set, who prefer 'safe' strategies, or by those who feel threatened. The management of change therefore requires some use of psychology. If you are now in a situation when you have identified the processes and directions of change and you wish to implement some major transformation within your organisation, you must understand that you need to move carefully. Beware stepping of on fragile egos. Change must be sensitively managed. But in the hands of someone with vision, change can create wonderful opportunities and open up startling new avenues for growth.

Agendas for change must come from the top. In your own business that means from you. You must take responsibility. Think, 'Unless I initiate the process, attitudes to change all the way down the line could well be negative. So I have to take responsibility and push.' This is because change *per se* is often perceived as threatening, and your far-sighted interests may not necessarily coincide with those of your senior staff or supporting personnel. This is especially the case when they can only see near-term scenarios, such as the possibility of their bonuses being affected by the initial reduction in sales perceived as arising from a change.

Sometimes resistance may come from unexpected quarters within your organisation, perhaps from your most dependable and longest-serving fellow director – not because she is against you, but because she does not understand what you envisage, nor appreciate your vision.

You must therefore invest some time to explain the rationale behind your proposals and actions – especially to your more trusted lieutenants. You require and need their support if you want any change initiated by you to succeed. Resistance to change also occurs when its process interferes with familiar patterns of behaviour and status. This can manifest itself as suspicion, fear and sometimes even outright hostility, especially when a change you implement takes place under conditions of uncertainty.

I remember when I had just started working for this family-owned Chinese group which desperately wanted to vault into the modern business world. The big boss decided to have a major restructuring of the whole company. There were so many pockets of resistance, mainly because so many of the general managers feared that under the new system they would lose their comfortable jobs or be transferred to other less important or less lucrative positions. It took great strength of purpose and determination – not to mention his own conviction of the need for the reorganisation – for the boss then to push through the changes he felt were needed to take his company into the next stage of its evolution and stay a major player in the new business environment.

Those of you contemplating this issue of change would do well therefore to understand that the management of the mechanism, the process and the pace of change will always pose enormous challenges. It helps if you set out substantial time for interactive discussions to perfect your rationale for change. Your goals should be clearly articulated. You should resolve all ambiguities. And you must obtain the fullest support of all your key staff – through persuasion or coercion.

Only then will the pace of change gather real momentum and you will be implementing your vision within an environment of support. This will reinforce your chances of success as your staff will then help you to fine-tune the process of change. You will also gain much needed confidence if you have the full support of your staff, because then there will be a widespread feeling of optimism within your organisation. Successful implementation of a change in direction will point to greater strength for the future. You will be adding building blocks of success, that will help you leapfrog into a much bigger league.

In the next chapter, which will be the final chapter, we shall focus on other issues that begin to take up more and more of your time as you continue on your way towards achieving multi-millionaire status. By now, at this stage of the game, you are no longer an entrepreneur. You will be starting to build the foundations for becoming a real bona fide tycoon!

Chapter Twelve

PRESERVING THOSE MILLIONS

There are very few 'highs' that can match the high of genuine achievement. The air up there at the top of the mountain is breathtakingly light. Knowing you are worth millions, and knowing you did not inherit or steal those millions, that they were not given to you, that you actually made them by your very own efforts is the one feeling every high-achieving person deserves to experience at least once in a lifetime.

But of course those millions were never an end in themselves. They were always a means to many ends – to be financially independent; to dine in the best restaurants; to travel the world in style; buy anything you fancy; to be dressed by top designers; to be driven around by a chauffeur; to be comfortable in all the smart places; to be looked up to, respected and recognised. All this is the stuff of dreams, the trimming that adorns the life and times of a successful well-heeled person.

Perhaps now is a good time to draw up a personal balance sheet. What can you list on the debit and credit sides? What are your *personal* assets and liabilities? How much did it cost you in terms of sacrifices to get to be a millionaire?

Stocktaking of this kind should feature prominently in the lives of successful people everywhere. Once you have accomplished what you set out to achieve, and especially when the objective was to have a great deal of money in the bank, future goals take on dramatic new perspectives.

The prospect of climbing further, to take on a higher or different mountain, to face further challenges, elicits different responses from different people. Depending on what stage of life you are at, you will react differently. As every successful person will tell you, it is never easy to match, let alone surpass, previous triumphs.

CHOOSING THE 'SAFER' OPTION

I know many self-made men and women, who, having built their business empires successfully, cashed in their profits by selling out. After a couple of years' sabbatical, some were attracted back to the corporate life – but with a difference. In their more mature years, these people opted for the 'safer' path of working for a corporation as an employee. The tough role of the risk-taker, the entrepreneur, no longer felt comfortable. Having made their millions, these people focused on preserving what they already had, allowing the capital sum created to grow via safe investments, while a salary took care of day-to-day expenses. The urge to get back into working life was satisfied by the (usually) high-powered job they took on.

It is usually women who opt for this less stressful path. My former partner, Cynthia Picazo, a Wharton MBA and former president of a finance company in Hong Kong, who joined forces with me in the Dragon Seed deal, stopped working for a couple of years after we sold out the company. Now she works as an executive director with a multinational company. She reverted back to the corporate life, but as an employee. Her millions are safely invested in blue-chip securities. The risk of a new venture is not for her.

I have no scientific statistics to make a definitive statement, but what I can tell you is that of my peers whose businesses did make it to the multi-million dollar level, the majority then sold out, stashing their money into 'safe' investments. These give steady returns which rarely eat into their capital sum.

It is easy to understand why mature and successful people become more averse to risk. With something tangible to lose, the impulsive decisiveness of their early years is seldom evident. Even in the management of their investments, I notice an inherent reluctance to risk losing what they have already made.

REACHING FOR THE SKY

For some, the urge to continue, to grow bigger, to grow richer is irresistible. Big businesses can be built around almost any industry – be it service-oriented or product-oriented. There is always room for 'upstarts' – medium-sized businesses that take on the corporate giants. There are always new ways of doing things – managing, producing, promoting, selling – and there are a zillion new ways to raise capital these days. For those with vision, the sky is the limit.

If you are at a stage where you are ready for a major expansion, you should examine some of the new methods of raising financing (see also pages 40–44). You can seriously consider listing your company on the stock exchange and 'inviting partners from the public' through an initial public offering (IPO). The requirements for listing on any board in any country do not seem so awesome or intimidating any more, especially when we hear of young twenty-something-year-olds suddenly being worth hundreds of millions of dollars, after listing companies started from the back of a garage.

The stories that leak out, especially from America, make everything seem enticingly within reach, and if you are already running a business whose turnover has reached the seven to eight-figure level, (and you have been consistently profitable), listing would be a super alternative to explore seriously. The stock market loves successful entrepreneurs who demonstrate potential . . . so do those professional money managers, the fund managers. It is worthwhile thinking about it. You could become seriously wealthy from the exercise.

Talk to a merchant bank. Contrary to popular belief, merchant banks do make time for successful entrepreneurial businesses that have reached the take-off stage. Indeed, if yours is a medium-sized business in a growth area (for instance in the Internet area), they simply *love* clients like you. Every professional corporate finance man or woman dreams of spotting the next Bill Gates or Larry Ellison.

If you are not sure whether your business would qualify, do not allow self-doubt to stop you from investigating the criteria for listing anyway. Talk to the corporate finance people of merchant banks. Something could come from it. Or just talk to business friends. You will be surprised how much you can pick up once you start investigating seriously.

If you are still doubtful, let me tell you a story. When Dickson Poon, the Hong Kong retail king, first met me, all he had were fifteen rented shops. Dickson was an ambitious man who harboured dreams of becoming the retail king of the world! He was young, clever and an extremely good businessman. I was very impressed by his perseverance and persistence. He had started his shops (selling watches, jewellery and other luxury products) with a HK$5 million loan from his father. Having built a successful chain of retail shops, he wanted to make a quantum leap, but didn't quite know how. I advised him to go public. We knew he did not have the asset base to get a listing, but once the idea got hold, he worked hard at getting that listing.

In those days, the 'backdoor listing' method was still fairly new. We found a listed company with some properties in it, then bought control of that company, after which Dickson injected his retail businesses into the listed company in exchange for that company's newly issued shares. Thus Dickson Concepts was born. I was the Executive Deputy Chairman of the company then.

Today, this company – now a billion-dollar worldwide retailing giant – owns full control of the luxury French firm, S.T. Du Pont of Paris (with over 500 boutiques worldwide) and also owns Harvey Nichols (with two major luxury department stores in the UK – in London and Leeds). So you potential Dickson Poons out there may very well be sitting on a potential goldmine, a potential conglomerate, a potential giant.

Do not place limits on your dreams and ambitions. If you have the stamina and possess the certainty of success, my advice to you is go for it. Allow yourself to be inspired by success stories. Read autobiographies of rich people who made their fortunes themselves. You will be surprised that these big-time successes also occasionally faltered and had their fears, worries and self-doubts.

Now that you have a bird's-eye view of all that is required of you when you embark on the quest to make your first million, go back to Chapter 1 and think again. Yes, if you have good ideas let the seed of them germinate. Don't let them die. Think of how you can enjoy your wealth when you have made it! That's what making money is about. To make your life, (and the lives of your loved ones) comfortable and meaningful.

Stay comfortable with the thought of making money and wanting to become rich. There is nothing bad and everything good about wanting to enjoy the fruits of materialism. Craving for wealth is not a bad thing, especially if you start out with the correct motivation, which is to generate the kind of independence that allows you to be your own person – better still, if your motivation is to use your life to help others. It is easier to be generous when you have the material things in life.

So examine your motivation. Aim to make your millions with a good heart.

APPENDIX I

DEVELOPING A SIGNATURE FOR SUCCESS WITH FENG SHUI

Your signature is said to attract success and prosperity if it starts with a firm upward stroke and ends with another firm upward stroke. Look at the following signatures:

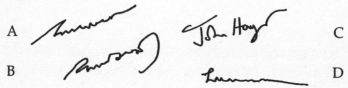

A   C

B   D

Signature A From a Feng shui perspective this will be the most auspicious signature of the four shown here.

Note the upward starting stroke and the upward ending stroke. This denotes a good beginning and a good ending to every project and job undertaken. My feng shui master tells me if you sign this type of signature forty-nine times on a wish list for forty-nine days, your wishes will come true.

Signature B This signature is only partly correct. It starts with a firm upward stroke, but it ends with an equally firm downward stroke. Signatures that seem to end with a backward movement are not auspicious. It indicates a sad ending.

Signature C This is another example of a signature that has excellent feng shui. Once again note that the beginning stroke is upward and the ending stroke is also upward. A line under a signature is also regarded as part of the signature. Thus those of you who do not have an upward ending stroke could include a firm line upwards to create the prosperity signature.

Signature D This signature has an almost unnoticeable downward slant to its ending. It is therefore not auspicious. If your signature looks like this, try to change it so the stroke is moving upwards.

FENG SHUI ADVICE FOR THOSE STARTING OUT IN BUSINESS

At work, while making all your business decisions, make sure you sit:

- in an auspicious orientation, facing a direction which brings you luck. You should check what this direction is according to the powerful Eight Mansions School of formula feng shui given in the table on page 173. Commit your auspicious directions to memory and always make sure you face the best one when working, negotiating or making a pitch.

- with something solid behind you, preferably a solid wall which can be further strengthened by hanging a picture of a mountain on it. This gives you solid support in your work. I would choose one of the three special mountains of the world, which are said to be three key chakras of the world. These are Mount Kailash in Tibet, Table Mountain in South Africa, and Ayers Rock in Australia. These mountains have a power of their own and their image would be ideal to place behind you.

- with the door clearly visible, either to the left or right, in front of you. If you sit with the door behind you, it is likely you could get cheated, taken for a ride or stabbed in the back – something you cannot afford to have happen to you at this stage of your working life.

MORE FENG SHUI ADVICE FOR NEW BUSINESSES

Don't forget to check that you are not sitting:

- directly beneath an exposed overhead beam, which could cause you to succumb to pressures and long hours at your desk. If you are, just move your desk out of the way.
- directly in the line of fire from the sharp edge of a protruding corner. If you are being 'hit' by such an edge, place a plant in front of the edge to soften its effects and move the desk a little bit to get it out of the way.

HARMONY IN THE OFFICE WITH FENG SHUI

You can ensure that everyone working with you interacts with each other in a harmonious and productive way by using a little bit of help from feng shui. An effective feng shui feature is to place a group of six smooth, natural crystal balls in the north-west corner of your office. This taps into the heavenly luck of networking and smooth inter-relationships. If you wish, you can also place more crystals in the south-west corner of your office. This is especially effective in companies that are headed by women, since energising the feng shui *chi* of south-west benefits the matriarchal energy.

IMPROVING THE FINANCIAL SITUATION OF YOUR BUSINESS WITH FENG SHUI

- Invest in a few Chinese coins, those that have a square hole in the centre. Then tie three coins together with red thread and attach these feng shui coins to your invoice or order book and your fax machine or computer.

- One of the best symbols you can introduce into the office to enhance your business luck is a model of a merchant sailing ship. I recommend using this symbol very strongly indeed, as it represents a bountiful cargo brought to you by wind and water. Since feng shui is about wind and water, the symbolic significance is enormously auspicious. Try to find a ship that is made of wood and which does not have cannons sticking out of its side. Then place semi-precious stones and simulated ingots and coins on its decks. Make very sure the ship is placed with the sails indicating that it is sailing *into* the office. If the ship is inadvertently turned to sail out, your profits will surely take a dive!

USING THE MAGIC OF THE WINDS TO BRING YOU YOUR MILLIONS

A famous Taoist master from Hong Kong once gave me a wish-list ritual, which he said would enhance business luck:

- Write down whatever you want the most on a helium-filled balloon. Write your wishes clearly and succinctly. Then release the balloons and let them fly high into the sky. It isn't feng shui by any means – it is a mind ritual that is such fun to do.

  One Sunday I did it and wrote down my wish to

be able to shop like a queen in all the capitals of the world. That was just before I completed the Dragon Seed deal (see page 103), which enabled me to have my own chain of department stores and to shop like an empress for two years, when I was Executive Chairman.

- A variation is to tie a banner with your wishes written on it across your garden. Let the winds carry your wishes into the sky to be realised for you.

ENHANCING YOUR CHANCES OF A PROFITABLE ACQUISITION

To enhance your chances of making a stunningly profitable acquisition that brings instant financial benefits for you or your company, I strongly recommend that you introduce the dragon fish or arrowana into your office. The best way to keep these wonderful feng shui fish is to import one from the dragon-fish farms of Singapore. It is not necessary to keep more than a single fish and because they grow rather fast, you should get a fairly large tank for it. Do not put any decoration (stones, grass, background) into the tank. The dragon fish needs nothing, save a powerful oxygenator to ensure the water gets aerated sufficiently. Usually the dragon fish feeds on live bait, but I would strongly suggest that you obtain specially made pellets (developed by aquarium enthusiasts in Germany).

Place your dragon-fish tank in the north or south-east corner of the office. It would be most auspicious to place it in the foyer or lobby of your office. Please make certain that you maintain the water properly and that it is kept clean at all times.

IMPROVING A SELL-OUT DEAL WITH FENG SHUI

When you are thinking of selling a business and want to find a buyer, use feng shui to energise for a lucrative deal. Activate the south-east corner of your office with either a nice big growing plant or install a fish tank and introduce the water element to this area of the office.

This will create vital yang energy for the sector that is associated with wealth.

PROTECTING YOUR BUSINESS WITH FENG SHUI

When your working life is moving along smoothly and all is well, it is not a bad idea to place some protective symbols around the office to 'seal' in the good fortune and protect against the onslaught of misfortunes that are caused by bad flying stars. This takes care of the time dimension of feng shui manifestations.

Set up a windchime to press down on the bad luck caused by the annual five-yellow inauspicious star. To do this successfully, you need to know where the five-yellow is located each year. In 1999, it was located in the south and windchimes had to be placed in that sector to guard against losses and illness in the office. In the year 2000, the five-yellow flies to the north, in 2001 to the south-west, in 2002 to the east, in 2003 to the south-east, in 2004 to the centre of the office and in 2005 it flies to the north-west. So move your windchime around every year to overcome the bad effects of this feng shui affliction.

Protective feng shui can also be activated by the presence of two Fu dogs placed near the entrance of the office building. These protect against loss and guard you from being cheated or played out. Businesses always benefit from the presence of the Fu dog.

GOOD FENG SHUI FOR BUSINESS

The feng shui of a corporation usually reflects that of its Chief Executive. When the boss has good feng shui so will the company, division or branch he or she runs. Thus owner/presidents of companies should always endeavour to ensure that they enjoy good feng shui.

An excellent way of ensuring that there is good feng shui in the office is to ensure it is always well lit, not excessively bright but also not too dark. Both the office of the Chief Executive and the boardroom can be enhanced by being regular in shape, free of square pillars and protruding corners and having doors placed on all exposed shelves. Bookshelves and anything that protrudes outwards represent poison arrows and ideally these should always be covered up.

It is also useful to note that the most auspicious room on any office floor is located in the diagonally opposite corner to the entrance to that floor. Usually the deeper inside the building, the better feng shui the room is said to have.

APPENDIX II

THE EIGHT MANSIONS KUA FORMULA OF FENG SHUI

If you want to succeed in business, I strongly recommend that you use the feng shui Eight Mansions Kua formula for identifying your personalised lucky locations and directions. Calculate your Kua number by following the formula below, and then refer to the table for your most auspicious corners and directions. Please note that these are your lucky *locations* – the luckiest spots in any room, office or apartment for you. Sitting, sleeping or working in any of these four specific locations will generally bring you good luck, and protect you from bad luck.

DETERMINING YOUR KUA NUMBER

Using your lunar calendar year of birth (refer to a lunar calendar), add the last two digits. Keep adding the digits until you get a single digit number. Then:

- For men, deduct this number from 10. The result is your Kua number.
- For women, add this number to 5. The result is your Kua number.

If you get two digits keep adding until you reduce it to one digit, e.g. if you get the number 10, then 1+0=1; and if you get the number 14, the 1+4=5. Refer to the table overleaf to find out your auspicious locations.

Your Kua number	Your auspicious corners & locations in descending order of luck	Indicating if you are an *East* or *West* person
1	South-East, East, South, North	East
2	North-East, West, North-West, South-West	West
3	South, North, South-East, East	East
4	North, South, East, South-East	East
5	*Men*: North-East, West, North-West, South-West *Women*: South-West, North-West, West, North-East	West
6	West, North-East, South-West, North-West	West
7	North-West, South-West, North-East, West	West
8	South-West, North-West, West, North-East	West
9	East, South-East, North, South	East

LILLIAN TOO'S WEBSITE

Welcome to Lillian Too's world on the worldwide web. Visit her website at www.lillian-too.com and e-mail her if you need clarification of any aspect of this book, including feng shui practices.

Lillian also has a new website to explore at www.worldoffengshui.com with news about the latest feng shui developments.